Travels
WITH QUEEN VICTORIA

Travels
WITH QUEEN VICTORIA

HRH The Duchess of York
and Benita Stoney

WEIDENFELD AND NICOLSON

LONDON

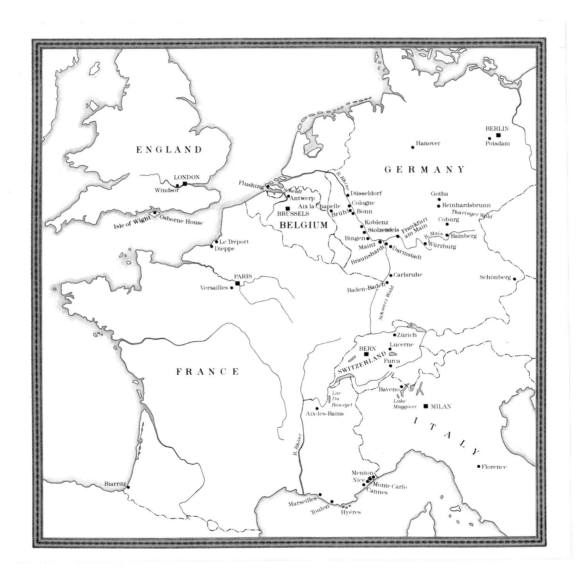

ENGLAND

LONDON
Windsor

Isle of Wight Osborne House

Le Tréport
Dieppe

PARIS
Versailles

FRANCE

Biarritz

Flushing
Scheldt
Antwerp
Aix la Chapelle
BRUSSELS
BELGIUM

R. Rhine

Düsseldorf
Cologne
Brühl Bonn
Koblenz
Stolzenfels Frankfurt
Bingen   am Main
Mainz
Braunshardt Darmstadt
Carlsruhe

Baden-Baden

Schwarz Wald

Zürich
Lucerne
BERN
Furca
SWITZERLAND

Lac Du Bourget
Aix-les-Bains

Baveno
Lake Maggiore MILAN

ITALY

Mentone
Nice Monte Carlo
Cannes
Marseilles
Toulon
Hyères

GERMANY

Hanover

BERLIN
Potsdam

Gotha
Reinhardsbrunn
Thüringer Wald
Coburg

R. Main Bamberg
Würzburg

Schönberg

Florence

R. Rhône

Contents

Foreword *page 6*

INTRODUCTION
Setting out from the
Royal Library at Windsor
page 10

CHAPTER ONE
Her Majesty's Plans
and Preparations
page 16

CHAPTER TWO
The Pilgrimage
to Coburg, 1845
page 48

CHAPTER THREE
The Land of
Albert's Birth, 1845
page 84

CHAPTER FOUR
The State Visit
to Paris, 1855
page 120

CHAPTER FIVE
The Delightful Fortnight,
Potsdam, 1858
page 138

CHAPTER SIX
The Late Holidays,
1861–1899
page 166

Family Tree
page 198

Reference Notes
page 200

Select Bibliography
page 202

Picture Acknowledgements
page 203

Index
page 204

Foreword

Queen Victoria has always fascinated me. I admire many of her qualities, and in some sense feel a bond of friendship with her. During the writing of *Victoria and Albert: Life at Osborne House*, when I learnt so much about her life, I discovered Queen Victoria's love of travel, which is echoed by the fascination for foreign parts and people which gently simmers in me. I was able to understand her longing to escape from the pressures of royal life and found her desire to broaden her horizons inspirational: I was spurred on to retrace her travels and to attempt to distill the spirit of her adventures. Guided by the Queen's detailed diaries, and accompanied by a band of merry travellers, I set out on a journey of discovery.

We began by visiting Coburg, for the first major journey that Queen Victoria made was with her beloved Albert to the land of his birth. When I arrived at the Rosenau, outside Coburg, where Albert was born on 26 August 1819, and where he brought his wife in 1845, the crisp, cloudless morning, with its blanket of sparkling frost, provided a magical welcome. I have always admired the Queen's devotion to Albert and the purity of her feelings for him, and this was where their captivating love story began. It felt like a dream to be following in their footsteps, and I had the sensation of being very close to them.

As I journeyed, the feeling continued. I found myself drawn to the very same view in Coburg as the Queen, looking down a narrow street to the market square; I wanted to paint the same building. Outside Nice I was seized with a sudden, very strong impulse to turn off the motorway and take the winding, mountainous road through La Turbie and Eze, going far out of my way through magical places, only to find later that, without realizing it, I had been following the route the Queen took. With hindsight, 'wrong turnings'

seemed to become a pattern, and I felt more certain that we were meant to visit these places. We passed the zoological gardens in Nice. I looked in the Queen's journal at the entry for 4 April 1895 and read that she drove there and saw that they were: 'really beautifully laid out and arranged, with such lovely palm and olive trees and every kind of shrub. The animals are fine specimens, though there are not a great number of them.' It was so exciting, and reassuring, to find my feelings were right. The following morning I woke up with the sun streaming through my open window. It was 7 a.m. and its warmth filled my room. I sat at breakfast on the terrace with an umbrella of pine trees providing the perfect shade. They seemed so comforting and friendly, as though offering an enduring link with the past; indeed, when I was on the train from Nice to Paris I read Queen Victoria's accounts of her trip to the area, where she described the same Cap Ferrat pine trees as 'umbrellas'.

The journals of Queen Victoria are a stimulating guide. She was always alert and observant, fascinated by the new places and different people she was seeing, and recorded her impressions in the greatest detail. It has been a delight to accompany her and to savour some of her enjoyment of the places she visited. She has taken us to areas which are little visited today; it seems that landscape as well as buildings are subject to the vagaries of taste and fashion. Travel has often been used as a metaphor for growth and the path towards realization and understanding. This trip was no exception.

I am deeply grateful to Her Majesty The Queen for having the kindness to allow Benita and me full access to the Royal Archives at Windsor Castle. All material from the Archives is published by gracious permission of Her Majesty.

I would like to give my heartfelt thanks to Allan Starkie for his continual support and help, and for his friendship. He influenced the development of this book through his dedication to helping me, through his breadth of vision, and through his amazing capacity to carry out his work while helping me with mine.

Benita and I would also like to thank Anna Delnef for her excellent organizing abilities and silent vigil, and Jane Dunn-Butler whose loyalty and kindness knows no bounds. Through his artful compositions photographer Robin Matthews superimposed the present upon the past with a skill which seemed to confuse time. His smiling face and unfailing kindness allowed his subject matter to appear calm. Stephanie Hornett's enthusiasm, support and constant caring glances reassured each and every one of us. Ahmet Eren drove our luggage through Germany and never lost track of us. Kate Waddington got us all to the right place at the right time. Martina Wilson gave support, and Jane Ambler never ceases in her unconditional loyalty and dedication to her job.

The Branca family in Baveno and the Maltzahns in Darmstadt were very generous hosts, as were the numerous curators and guides we encountered along the way. In Coburg Jürgen Mattstadt went far out of his way to help us, and Herr Appelsauer was most generous in relating the history of his town and its princes. In Bonn Ingeborg Krueger kindly gave us proofs of her article on Queen Victoria's visit. Throughout Germany, Roland Allen was an inspirational fellow-traveller. In Paris Rob and Catherine Young gave their enthusiastic support. In Aix-les-Bains, Aline Porcheron and Kim Hall provided lively details of the *belle époque*. At Grasse Roger Grihangne supplied plentiful detail on Queen Victoria's visit. The gentle gardeners at La Mortola were charming and hospitable. In England, Delia Millar gave invaluable advice and Ken Corden kindly made available to us Queen Victoria's paintbox which she presented to his great-grandfather, the painter William Corden, in 1862. At Windsor the staff of the Royal Library and Royal Archives, in particular Oliver Everett, Frances Dimond, Gwyneth Campling, Jane Roberts, Bridget Wright and Theresa Mary Morton were, as ever, unhesitatingly helpful, while Sheila de Bellaigue and Pamela Clark bore the brunt of our researches and queries.

Finally, we would like to think Lord Weidenfeld and Lord Mishcon who devised the idea, and of course the people who made it all happen: Michael Dover, our publisher, whose patience and tolerance are unequalled, Suzannah Gough, our editor, whose kindness and enthusiasm enabled the project to succeed, and Harry Green who created a masterful design with such joy and confidence.

Thank you all so very much for giving Benita and me a unique and wonderful opportunity to travel in time.

'In March when it was bleak and grey at home, Queen Victoria would go south for rest and balmy air. It was a much gentler way than ours, for we leave home for summer holidays when the weather is at its hottest. As well as her wise choice of seasons, Queen Victoria found kind, generous people who felt honoured to offer her their homes as a retreat. Mr Henfrey, the railway magnate, who owned the Villa Clara in 1879 offered his hospitality just as the present owners, Conte and Contessa Branca, did for me.'

Setting out from the Royal Library at Windsor

'Here, among the treasures in the Royal Library at Windsor, is the first exciting glimpse of the wonderful places I will soon be visiting. As I look through the albums which contain the paintings of many of the sights Queen Victoria and Prince Albert visited together, and the faint aroma of old books wafts up, I let my imagination go, slipping back to the time when all these leatherbound volumes were new, and I feel all the enthusiasm and anticipation of setting out: this is where my journey of discovery begins.'

In the hush of the Print Room in the Royal Library at Windsor Castle the light is subdued, the floor creaks softly under the red carpets, and sometimes there seem to be footsteps overhead even when there is no one around. The tall windows overlook a wide panorama where the river Thames sweeps past on its way from the shires to London. You are inside one of the landmarks of England.

The walls are shadowy, lined with high, glass-fronted cupboards which open with a little click as albums as big as paving slabs, bound in scarlet leather stamped with gold, are brought out and laid on the maroon table top in a pool of light.

Your hands seem very small as you lift open the great scarlet binding and turn back the tissue paper that interleaves the broad, creamy pages. Suddenly you find yourself looking through a window onto another world, at paintings of a forgotten Europe, distant and intense, like looking back at history through a telescope, bright with colour. Against soft blue distances of rivers and woods are palaces built of colour and light, large and airy, castles designed for fairytales, whose interiors are painted with such clarity that you feel you could step straight into them. You can sense the motes of dust hanging in the sunbeams that filter through the stained-glass windows. You feel you could run your hand over all the different textures in the rooms: the cool smoothness of silken furnishings, the furry warmth of red velvet, the deep gloss of a newly polished table, the rich blue pile of a carpet on the floor. As you turn the pages you seem to wander from room to room, and the questions begin: what is through that half-open door? where does this winding stair lead? You puzzle over the unfamiliar names – Brühl, Stolzenfels, Würzburg, Ehrenburg – as you

are lead through green landscapes of plump, wooded hills dotted with prosperous, brightly painted, red-roofed houses with garlands on their walls, and you ask, why the strange mixture: paintings of peasants in their traditional costumes next to paintings of great German baroque palaces?

Another massively heavy album comes out, revealing another series of magical paintings, this time of cavalcades and processions, fireworks, balls, al fresco luncheons and hunting parties. You can hear the cheering of the crowds and the clattering of the horses' hooves as the carriage processions roll by under banners of welcome streaming from foreign windows. Here you can snatch a quick rest in a blue and gold boudoir with a view of Paris in the distance; there you can hear the buzz of voices in candlelit ballrooms and an orchestra tuning up nearby, or the fizz and crack of fireworks as one monarch greets another with a brilliant display to the sound of guns.

In yet another album an old lady in a black bonnet is waited on by turbaned Indians and kilted Highlanders. Palm trees nod in the background, and she sets

As carefully preserved as any of the volumes in the Royal Library are Queen Victoria's own sketchbooks. Hers is a very personal record; in the two little books open here we see (left) a view in Coburg and (above) Zouaves from her escort in Paris, 1855. The paintbox also belonged to the Queen.

off for her afternoon's drive to the sound of bugles along a road built by Napoleon high above the Mediterranean.

These great volumes, as red as the tunics of the sentries outside Windsor Castle, are the souvenir albums of Queen Victoria. They were begun in the days when the Queen and Prince Albert travelled together, commissioning paintings of all the places they visited. When they came home they would

This magnificent album profusely decorated with gold tooling was presented to the Queen as a souvenir of her state visit to Paris in 1855. It contains photographs and illuminations showing the route of her journey from Boulogne to Paris.

spend nostalgic evenings arranging their mementoes in order, so that they had a complete record of all that they had seen.

Close to the souvenir albums is a low cupboard, heavily carved. Inside, rather worn and shabby, is a series of plain sketchbooks, some bound in green leather and some in red, stamped in gold 'VR'. They are filled with drawings, some abandoned almost as soon as begun, others carefully finished, and the best pasted into two larger albums bound in suede. These are Queen Victoria's own sketchbooks, some fifty of them. As you read the names she pencilled in beneath her sketches of picturesque peasants in their traditional headgear, of various views 'from my sitting room' and enthusiastic silhouettes of famous mountains, it becomes clear that Queen Victoria travelled a very great deal, far more than most people realize.

To make sense of many of the paintings, and to learn the story that went with them, we had to thread our way through the labyrinth of the Royal Archives, that great whispering gallery of the past, where the closed boxes, the folded papers and the fat red leather-bound volumes of royal letters unlock their secrets piecemeal – a fragment or a telegram here, a throw-away line in a letter there. As you tread the labyrinth, following the small clues that make up the story, you might unwrap a tightly folded bundle tied up with faded pink tape, or open a volume of letters written on blue paper with a heavy black edge, thick black ink hurrying across the pages in Queen Victoria's own emphatic hand. You imagine the letter being written, blotted, folded up. You imagine the Queen, seated at her writing table or perhaps in a garden wearing a little black apron to protect her silk dress from ink spots, at work on the vast correspondence which she dealt with day in, day out, whether she was at home in England or Scotland or away in Germany, France, Italy or Switzerland. You open the plain blue books containing her journal, but here the hand is different: it is that of her youngest daughter, Beatrice, to whom the Queen bequeathed her private papers. Beatrice rewrote the Queen's entire journal, which runs to over a hundred volumes, burning the original as she went along. You read it through the filter of her daughter's editing, but the Queen's character is so strong that she comes through in all her contradictions, certainties and uncertainties, and strenth and enjoyment of all the new places she was seeing.

In November 1992, when Windsor Castle caught fire, much was destroyed, and tragic pictures of the wreck of St George's Hall went round the world, but the Royal Library and Royal Archives, with their insight into the ways of the past, survived intact, and allow us the privilege of opening this magic casement onto a vanished era.

Queen Victoria's journal for 16 September 1843, copied by her daughter, with a sketch by the Queen of a Belgian bishop. The Queen was describing a visit to her uncle Leopold, King of the Belgians.

CHAPTER ONE

Her
Majesty's
Plans and Preparations

*A
Timetable
of the
Travels*

The child who became Queen Victoria was born in England, but only just. Her parents were married at Kew in 1818. Her father was Edward Duke of Kent, a younger son of George III, and her mother was Victoria, widow of the Prince of Leiningen but by birth of the house of Saxe-Coburg. When the duchess was newly pregnant she and her husband set out for Germany and, because the Duke was unable to borrow enough money to return to England, became stranded there until the duchess was eight months gone. He wanted the child, who would be heir to the English throne, to be born in England, and with true heroism the duchess made the arduous return journey in a carriage driven by her husband, and reached England on 23 April 1819. Only a month later, on 24 May, the little princess was born. With such odysseys in her very blood it was little wonder that Queen Victoria grew to love travelling.

She remained in her own kingdom until after her marriage to Prince Albert of Saxe-Coburg in 1840. Her first excursion abroad was in September 1843, when she and Prince Albert visited Louis-Philippe, the 'Citizen King' of France. He entertained her in a modest way with *fêtes-champêtres* at the Château d'Eu, which was conveniently near the coast of France, close to Le Tréport, and

Queen Victoria's first foreign excursion was to France, when she visited King Louis-Philippe at the Château d'Eu in 1843. In 1855, during the Crimean War, she paid a state visit to the Emperor Napoleon III; the watercolour opposite by Antoine Leon Morel-Fatio shows her arrival at Boulogne (detail).

Luncheon at Sainte
Catherine à Garde-
Chasse, Forest of Eu,
6 September 1843; the
King of France entertains
the Queen of England.
(Watercolour by S. Fort.)

Her Majesty was reported to be 'as amused as a child could be, and very much pleased with her reception'.[1] It was quite an historic occasion, for it was the first time that the English sovereign had met the French since Henry VIII and Francis I had met on the Field of the Cloth of Gold.

A few days later the Queen and Prince Albert went to see their Uncle Leopold, King of the Belgians. After several days of relentless sightseeing in Bruges and Ghent – libraries, town halls, picture collections, convents, cathedrals, concerts and theatres – they made a grand 'entrée' into Antwerp, stayed in Uncle Leopold's palace at Laecken, attended more concerts, watched a procession of giants, visited the cathedral, slept in a bed that had belonged to Napoleon and Marie Louise, saw modern pictures, works by Rubens and Rubens's tomb, and departed to cheering crowds and bands. 'Tired, I own I was', admitted the Queen who had a constitution of iron, 'but so interested and pleased, with all I had seen, and I feel how much (as Albert said one day) I shall profit by having been in other countries.'[2]

She was very taken with travel, and in 1845 her favourite dream was realized: on 20 August she joyfully awoke in the Rosenau outside Coburg, in the very house in which Albert had been born. Here they spent a happy week before going on to Gotha. The Queen had wished to see the places which were so familiar to her through her mother and through Albert, who were both brought up at Coburg, and this visit to Coburg and Gotha was primarily a family affair, but on the way the royal couple paid a visit to the King of Prussia and on the way home they again called in on Louis-Philippe. Le Tréport was not at all convenient as a port, and on this occasion, as the tide was out, the royal

barge had to be rather ignominiously towed ashore by a bathing machine. The whole journey, however, was considered a great success: 'one of the most beautiful journeys we have ever made', wrote Prince Albert afterwards.[3] The Queen returned 'delighted' and 'quite enchanted'.[4]

The frequent arrival of children (between November 1840 and May 1850 Queen Victoria had seven), the acquisition of two new homes, Osborne and Balmoral, and the upheavals in Europe which culminated in 1848, the Year of Revolutions, meant that it was some years before Victoria and Albert ventured

Arrival of Queen Victoria at the Château d'Eu. (Watercolour by Eugene Lami.) 'I feel very gay and amused by everything', wrote the Queen in her journal for 4 September. 1843.

abroad again, once more for a brief family visit to King Leopold in 1852.

Altogether a different affair was the brilliant state visit to Paris in 1855, undoubtedly one of the most glamorous events of the Queen's life, to which we shall return in Chapter 4.

Her children were growing up fast: the two eldest, Victoria, the Princess Royal, known in the family as Vicky, and the Prince of Wales, Bertie, were old enough to accompany their parents to Paris. Three years later Vicky married Prince Frederick William of Prussia (Fritz) and went to live in Berlin. The Queen was not long in following, to see for herself her daughter's new home. She spent a 'delightful fortnight'[5] in August 1858 at Schloss Babelsberg, known as the Prussian Versailles, in Potsdam, outside Berlin.

Fifteen years after Queen Victoria's first visit to Coburg with Albert they returned there, in the autumn of 1860, and were joined by Vicky with their first grandchild, Prince William of Prussia. It would always be family matters which would bring the Queen to Coburg. At this stage in her life she was already revisiting her own past. She saw again Stolzenfels, where she had stayed with the King of Prussia in 1845, 'and went entirely over this really beautiful place. I remembered so well the rooms we had and everything reminded me so often of the poor king.'[6] Gloomy portents cast threatening shadows over the visit. En route they received news of the death of Albert's stepmother, the Dowager Duchess of Coburg, and on 1 October Albert was involved in a bad carriage accident at a level crossing just outside Coburg. He jumped clear, but was bruised and shocked. The coachman was badly injured and one of the horses killed. The departure of the Queen and Prince was delayed to give Albert time to recover completely.[7] Just before he left Coburg he confessed, weeping, that he feared he would never see his birthplace again. The following year, 1861, he died.

The death of Albert was a watershed in the Queen's life; nothing was ever the same again. When she lost the man who was everything to her the world turned upside down; for many years all that had been pleasant or

Queen Victoria's journal open at her vivid description of the glacier at the source of the Rhône, 23 August 1868.

fun became a torment to her, reminding her unbearably of 'former happy times'. Life became a burden. But she still travelled, casting about for ways of easing her grief, and spent the autumn of 1862 at Reinhardsbrunn, a hunting lodge belonging to the Duke of Coburg on the edge of the Thüringer Wald; one of the places she had liked best in 1845, it was a comforting mix of Scottish and German not unlike Balmoral. She stayed there for five weeks, steeling herself, as it were, to revisit Coburg, the place which had meant so much to both of them. The peaceful Rosenau only intensified her sorrow. On the way home she called in on Uncle Leopold and became stormbound. Without

Statue of Prince Albert erected by his grieving widow in Coburg. The Queen, deeply moved, was present at its unveiling: 'the signal was given and in one second the drapery fell away from the statue, which stood there, in all its beauty, so sad and grand.' Her journal for the day, 26 August 1865, concludes, 'I was very tired when I got back, feeling inexpressibly sad and lonely'.

Albert Laecken had entirely lost its lustre: 'Oh!' she cried, 'and here I am with all the children all alone without beloved Papa's council and advice and love and feel lonely and so wretched, in this terribly dull place – where really I feel as if one would lose one's intellects.'[8]

1863 saw her unhappily in Coburg again and in 1865, when she spent three and a half weeks at the Rosenau, she was present for the unveiling of the prince's statue in Coburg's market square.

For the next few years war prevented her from travelling, but in 1868 times were settled enough to allow her to go to Switzerland; Albert having seen the

The Villa Friesenberg at Baden-Baden, 1865, with Queen Victoria's half-sister, Feodore, Princesss of Hohenlohe-Langenburg, standing on the lawn. Queen Victoria first visited 'dearest Feodore's charming little villa in the chalet style' on 26 March 1872. She herself stayed here in 1876 and 1880.

Alps, she wished to do so too. She stayed at the Pension Wallis in Lucerne, and made an expedition up the St Gotthard Pass to Furca. She saw the Matterhorn, marmots and the glacier, 'like something unearthly! The road descends in 7 great zig zags and with this marvellous glacier piled up in huge boulders of solid ice, with peaks like rocks, looked so alarming and steep.'[9] She stayed at what she called a desolate little inn, the Hotel Furca, and the next day went 'to the foot of the glacier, where the Rhône runs out from underneath it, in a thick white stream' and sat down for tea 'on the grass under a small bank, watching the water boil in a *casserole*, a *kettle* being unknown in these parts'.[10]

It was four years before she could travel again, in the spring of 1872, in the aftermath of the Franco-Prussian War. She saw from the train at Strasbourg the signs of the 'fearful struggle' of the autumn of 1870.[11] She was on her way to visit her half-sister, Feodore of Hohenlohe-Langenburg in Baden-Baden, really the first place she visited which had no connection with Albert. Indeed, newly widowed, she had once replied to a suggestion of Vicky's, 'Baden would never do; dear Papa had a horror of it.'[12] The spa town had long been a playground for the rich and fashionable who came to take the waters, but the Queen came 'quietly' in the spring, avoiding the Season with its gambling, horse-races, concerts, *demi-monde*, kings and emperors. She stayed in the Villa Delmar, 'situated a little above the town with a small garden and surrounded by villas ... quite pretty looking but rather showy'.[13] The house was furnished 'like a French château and not quite to my taste'.[14] The town was 'most picturesque quite overhung by wooded hills'[15] and the Black Forest, with its magnificent silver firs and spruces, made for such 'delicious' driving.[16] Her half-sister died soon afterwards, leaving her house to the Queen, who would have liked to return in 1875 to visit the grave and see the 'beautiful monument' to which she had contributed, but was prevented from doing so on account of her haemophiliac son, Prince Leopold, falling ill.[17] She renamed the house the Villa Hohenlohe, and stayed there 'with what sad feelings' in 1876 (when she also visited Coburg) and in 1880.

Queen Victoria first visited Italy in 1879, staying on the shores of Lake Maggiore in the Italian lake district. She later made three visits to Florence. In 1888 and 1893 she stayed at the Villa Palmieri in Fiesole, lent to her by Lady Crawford, from which she had a fine view of the city, and in 1894 at the Villa Fabbricotti. She 'delighted' in the Ponte Vecchio, the Pitti Palace she thought 'magnificent', and the Uffizi contained 'the most marvellous collection'. She was less enthusiastic, however, about the Piazza Michelangelo, 'with a colossal statue of David copied from the original by Michael Angelo, with four statues round it. I do not admire it.'[18] She reacted indignantly, and rather defensively, to a suggestion of Vicky's: 'You are quite wrong', she insisted, 'if you think I do not care for art. I delight in it. Only I can't spend hours upon it, as you can, or go about everywhere. I am enchanted with the pictures.'[19] Nevertheless, the Queen describes much more vividly the things she really enjoyed, like the Easter tradition known as Scoppio del Carro, in which a mechanical dove conveyed 'holy fire' from the altar of the *duomo* to a cart in the square drawn by white oxen; it also involved, the Queen explained, 'a trelliswork of fireworks. From the car to the High Altar in the Cathedral, a wire is stretched along which the artificial dove flies, with what is called holy fire in its mouth. After waiting $\frac{1}{4}$ of an hour, out came the dove with a sudden whiz, and as quickly went back again, whereupon the fireworks exploded with a tremendous noise.'[20]

Queen Victoria first set eyes on the Mediterranean in 1882, when she stayed at Menton, renowned for its mild climate. She loved it, although, like Baden-Baden, it had its undesirable aspects: 'One saw very nasty disreputable looking people walking about at Monte Carlo, though many respectable people go

Queen Victoria visiting the church of the Santissima Annunziata in Florence on 11 April 1893. (Ink and wash by A. Forestier.) When she grew stiff and rheumaticky the old Queen would allow herself to be wheeled around in a little chair.

A street in Chambéry looking towards Grenoble. (Watercolour by Gabriel Carelli.) The Queen could visit Chambéry, 'the position of which is beautiful and the town picturesque' (7 April 1890), on her daily drives while she was staying at Aix-les-Bains.

there also for their health. The harm this attractive gambling establishment does, cannot be overestimated.'[21] From then on her spring holiday, generally in France, was virtually an annual event. Ten years later she was an expert on southern resorts: Aix-les-Bains, then a fashionable spa town, which she had visited in 1885, 1887 and 1890, was 'beautiful and quite in the mountains but the vegetation is not very southern, no orange trees or palms or stone pines and it is often very cold at the end of March and very backward. Therefore I don't so readily go there.'[22] Biarritz, where she stayed in 1889 in a villa belonging to Baron de la Rochefoucauld, was 'not a nice or pretty place, very bleak and very barren with a constant high wind and no vegetation. The sea is very grand to see in a storm and there are many interesting recollections of the Visigoths but I would never care to go there again.'[23] Grasse (1891) was grand and wild, but there were fewer drives and the vegetation was not so fine as at Hyères (1892), which was 'much more private and quiet and very pleasant'.[24] In this sweeping summary Queen Victoria does not seem to have thought Cannes, where she stayed in 1887 at the Villa Edelweiss, the property of a Mr A. Lumley, to have been worth mentioning, though at the time she had exclaimed over Cannes spread before her, 'endless multitudes of villas built up the sides of the hills, above the railway surrounded by gardens and grounds full of palm trees, eucalyptus, magnolias, mimosa, aloes, orange trees with fruit on them, – quite marvel-

LEFT: Queen Victoria's journal for 16 March 1882, the day she first set eyes on the 'far famed' Mediterranean.

OPPOSITE: Queen Victoria seated on the balcony of the Grand Hotel at Grasse, watching the cavalcade of the Battle of Flowers on 30 March 1891. Princess Beatrice can be seen making a donation. The Queen thought the procession 'a very original and amusing sight'.

ABOVE: Fashionable yachts lying in the harbour below the old town of Menton, March 1898.

lous'.[25] The last of her holidays, from 1895 to 1899, were spent at Cimiez, an elevated suburb of Nice. In 1900, during the Boer War, she did not go abroad as she felt that it would be inappropriate to take a southern holiday.

Dynastic concerns, of course, still called her back to Germany, as in 1888, when she went to Berlin in a fairly hostile anti-English climate, and against all advice, to pay her last respects to the new emperor. Her son-in-law, Fritz, had inherited the throne as a dying man. She interviewed Prince Bismarck – 'a most interesting conversation' from which the Iron Chancellor is reported to have emerged mopping his brow – and drove through the streets of cheering crowds: force of personality carried the day, backed up by the prestige of personifying a world power. She made her seventh, and last, journey to Coburg in 1894, after her second son had become Duke of Coburg, to see two of her grandchildren marry one another. It was a match of the Queen's making, and a disaster.

OPPOSITE: Queen Victoria in a phaeton in the grounds of the Villa Liserbe at Cimiez, April 1898.

So regular were Queen Victoria's visits abroad that she considered buying a holiday property herself. She did in fact purchase land with a view to building at Tresserve, a hillside outside Aix-les-Bains, overlooking the Lac du Bourget and made famous by the poet Lamartine. In the end, however, she decided against it; she enjoyed trying out new places too much to tie herself down.

Plans and Preparations

Since the Queen was head of state, the business of reigning had to go on more or less as usual even while she was abroad, and she could not be out of the country for too long. Before she and Prince Albert went to Coburg in 1845 the prince warned his brother that they would have to hurry: 'We must not stay away much more than three weeks. Otherwise a Regency must be appointed.'[26] On that occasion they were away for four weeks, but no regency was ever appointed while the Queen was on her travels. It was sometimes a difficult business to get the timing right, but it was for others to compromise, not Her Majesty, as we can see in this letter from the Queen to the Prime Minister, Disraeli, in 1875:

> She is anxious *this next year*, to go abroad *for three* weeks, (journey included) to Baden and Coburg, about Easter time . . . the only inconvenience, is that Easter is very late and that therefore the Queen, will be unable to take in the whole fortnight of the Parliamentary Easter Vacation as she naturally wishes to be back a *full month*, before coming *here* [Balmoral] for the spring visit. The last time the Queen went abroad in *72* at Easter, Parlt *was* sitting, for a few days, and though this would be *rather* longer, she trusts that with the arrangement made by the Lord Chancellor in 1868, that it could easily be managed . . . she would therefore be thankful, if Mr Disraeli could arrange to have Parliament opened *as late as possible*.[27]

She chose to go in the spring for travelling in the summer 'disagreed with her *so very much* on account of the great heat'.[28] Besides being more comfortable for her, it meant that she went to fashionable places at a quiet time of year, always an essential. Just as she went unseasonably early in the year to Baden-Baden, where the Season ran from May to October, with royalty usually coming in September and October, so she went in March to Aix-les-Bains, which, 'as usual at this season', reported *The New York Herald*, 'is almost deserted'.[29] According to *The Times*, 'Only a very small number of the 40 hotels and 18 boarding houses which Aix contains, are open, and the few which are nominally so have few visitors, excepting the Hotel de l'Europe, where the Queen herself is staying'.[30] The Queen's arrival would bring a few early visitors, mostly English, but the Season in Aix really began in May. In the south of France, where the winter months were the busy ones and most hotels were closed in the summer, she arrived at the end of the Season.

When the Queen of England visited another European country it was taken for granted that its people would wish to greet her with all due honours, and

Queen Victoria on holiday at Aix-les-Bains, 10 April 1890: 'Went out in the garden where we found Arthur's children being photographed. Was done with them.' Left to right: Princess Margaret of Connaught, Queen Victoria, Prince Henry of Battenburg, Princess Patricia and Prince Arthur of Connaught, the Marquess of Lorne and Princess Beatrice. (Photograph by Numa Blanc Fils.)

would expect a public response from her. Long ago Albert had advised, 'It would not be good policy to prevent the people from showing their pleasure at seeing us.'[31] Popular enthusiasm had to be taken into account when plans were being made, as in 1860 when her Uncle Leopold had written to the Queen, 'It will be most kind if you let me know the exact time of your return [from Coburg]. Some of our towns want to display loyalty in October but I declined fixing the days before I was informed of your will and pleasure.'[32] In the early days the Queen travelled to a barrage of cheering crowds and gun salutes, with bunting along every route; on her journey to Babelsberg for instance she saw 'everywhere decorations, flags, flowers, the engine even being decorated, and the stations, very prettily'.[33]

Her Majesty's expressed wish to travel incognito has been all in vain, said the newspapers reporting her visit to Berlin. After Albert's death all that changed, however, and she really did travel as quietly and privately as possible:

From Villa Clara Baveno looking towards Stresa. April 1879

Watercolour painted by the Queen while staying on Lake Maggiore, inscribed 'From Villa Clara Baveno looking towards Stresa, April 1879'. Here, she said, one could sketch all day and never be satisfied with the result.

no salutes, no guards of honour, no bands, no flags, no official receptions. In the distress of bereavement her nerves would not stand the aggravation. She generally travelled under one of her lesser titles, as in 1862, when she made the first journey of her widowhood as the Duchess of Lancaster.[34] For a while she used the title Countess of Kent, but because her son Prince Alfred was Earl of Kent she could not continue to use it after he married. In 1879 she decided upon Countess of Balmoral, 'which will sound very pretty'.[35]

The incognito was always transparent, and by the end of her long travelling career had worn away entirely. She was received in Florence in 1894 by, as she said, 'great crowds, much clapping of hands and kind faces of welcome'.[36] She

Queen Victoria's arrival at the Villa Fabbricotti, Florence, 16 March 1894. (Photograph by Flli. Alinari.)

would be greeted in France in the 1890s, one of her Household later remembered, by:

a dense crowd of people who waved and cheered. The British were not popular at that time with the French, but I never saw anything but enthusiasm for the Queen. On the pier was a beautiful red velvet and gold lace tent for her to sit in, with a guard of honour of the French Army, while a host of Generals, Admirals, and officials hoping to be presented were drawn up near the tent. What with the band playing and the crowd continually cheering vociferously, it was difficult to hear anything.[37]

Who
and What
to
Take

The Queen having decided where, when and as whom she was going, who accompanied her? In 1845 it had been fairly simple. For 'Society', as he called it, Prince Albert proposed taking six tried and tested travelling companions who, as he said, having the previous autumn 'lived with us in a miserable small house in Scotland' and 'made very merry', could be trusted 'not to make any pretentions'.[38] Those who went were two lords, Aberdeen and Liverpool (Secretary of State for Foreign Affairs and Lord Steward respectively), the prince's secretary, Mr Anson, an equerry, Colonel Wylde, and two ladies-in-waiting, Lady Canning and Lady Gainsborough. As an additional precaution the Queen also took her doctor, Sir James Clarke.

For the visit to Paris, which was not a family but a state affair, more show was necessary. Extra officials were included in the retinue, which consisted of two ladies-in-waiting, one maid of honour, the Lord Chamberlain, the Secretary of State for Foreign Affairs, the Groom of the Stole to the prince, the Clerk Marshal, the equerry-in-waiting and secretary to the prince (two offices, one person), the Keeper of the Privy Purse, the Master of the Household, the physician to the Queen and, for the children, the governess to the Princess Royal and the tutor to the Prince of Wales.

The servants, Albert had said, unravelling this knotty problem in 1845, 'are always the most difficult question, but we shall try to take those who are Germans with us. They know how things are in Germany.'[39] Today, to work out the number of servants who accompanied the royal party is still 'the most difficult question' because no one ever thought they were worth recording, unlike 'Society'. The Queen does name four who went to Coburg and Gotha in 1845,[40] besides whom the prince would almost certainly have had his valet, Cart, who had been with him since childhood, and quite possibly his outdoor servant, Löhlein, whom he had also brought with him from Germany, making a possible total of six. There would have been other servants besides, for when Lady Canning went to France with the Queen in 1843 she and the other lady-in-waiting each brought a maid with them.[41]

By 1890, however, when the Queen was travelling with her daughter Princess Beatrice and her husband, the number of the accompanying retinue was up round the forty mark. Of these, only the three members of the royal family and ten others were deemed grand enough to appear by name on the official list of foreigners arriving at Aix-les-Bains; the rest were listed simply as 'and suite'. Four of the ten people named were Her Majesty's Indian attendants. The Queen also took her Highland attendants. Even housemaids went. One of

Hôtel de Ville, Paris: entrance to the Galerie des Glaces. (Watercolour by Arthur Diets.) Glamorous occasions such as this one, which took place during the Queen's visit to Paris in 1855, required meticulous behind-the-scenes organization. On the first evening of the visit two of the Queen's ladies-in-waiting were unable to attend dinner because the luggage containing their dresses had not arrived.

them, Elizabeth Reynolds, died of septicemia during the visit to Grasse. The Queen repaired to 'the Cemetery of St Brigitte, to find a quiet sunny spot' and made a sketch of what she wished to be placed over the grave: 'It is to be a simple white cross, with a little railing round it, and I have bought the ground.'[42] She was very upset by the death, and took the keenest interest in the obsequies. Her Household, composed of 'Society', thought she was going too far: 'Of course I admire the Queen for taking such a lively interest in her servants', wrote a maid of honour, 'but it is overdone in this sort of way and it is very trying for the Household.'[43] The white cross can still be seen in the cemetery.

By about 1894, according to the Queen's assistant private secretary, 'altogether, counting the Princesses and the suite there were about a hundred to be transported from England'. A list of all the servants was submitted to the Queen who 'said she had gone carefully into it and found she could not do without one of them'.[44] All in all, when Her Majesty could sit, as at Menton, enjoying the peace and write 'the night quite splendid, – many stars, not a sound to be heard',[45] a lot of people were holding their breath.

Transporting such an army required military powers of organization, or at least the cool, orderly mind of a Prince Albert, who planned the journey to Coburg and Gotha. In those early days arrangements were made on a relatively *ad hoc* basis. For the return journey from Gotha Albert sent on ahead an experienced servant, Teckely, who had been his father's valet for twenty years, to the Kurfurst Hotel in Fulda, the Hotel d'Angleterre in Frankfurt and the Hotel Bellevue at Deutz 'to take our rooms for us' which, as the Queen afterwards explained, 'he had done extremely well'.[46] For the trip to Berlin in 1858 the courier charged a fee of £60, and his expenses, which including preliminary journeys, came to £78.12s.[47]

In 1860 Her Majesty took a permanent courier into her service.[48] As well as making arrangements for the Queen, Joseph Julius Kanné arranged the journeys of the sickly Prince Leopold to Cannes in 1861[49] and of the Prince of Wales to the Middle East in 1862.[50] Kanné was with Prince Alfred in Germany in 1864[51] and was Prince Arthur's courier to Paris in 1867,[52] accompanying him to Rome in 1873. In 1874 he arranged the voyage to St Petersburg of the Prince and Princess of Wales and Prince Arthur, and in the same year, as Director of Continental Journeys, was presented with the Victoria Faithful Service Medal for fourteen years' service.[53] He flits in and out of the Queen's journal, appearing in 'a great state of fright to hurry us on'[54] as darkness was falling on the St Gotthard Pass, and again on 24 April 1888 when she received news of his death: 'For thirty years', she wrote, 'he had attended me on all my journeys, making all the arrangments in a most admirable manner. He used to think of every little thing for my pleasure and comfort and had a wonderful power of organisation.'[55] His place was taken by Ernest Dosse.

One of the courier's concerns would have been arranging transportation of the quantities of luggage that accompanied the Queen on her travels. In the early days baggage was frequently delayed en route, even though servants would be sent off with it hours in advance of the Queen's crack-of-dawn starts. At Schloss Brühl in 1845 there arose 'a hue and cry for a huge travelling basket of the Queen's' in which, Lady Canning believed, lived 'combs, brushes, shoes, stockings, books, sugar plums, writing paper etc.'.[56] A few days later at Würzburg, one of the most splendid palaces in Germany, the Queen passed 'a somewhat uncomfortable evening, as some of our people and most of our luggage did not arrive, so we had to settle for the night as best we could'.[57] Even on the state visit to Paris in 1855 the Queen recorded that 'Many of our things had not come', so two of her ladies were unable to appear at dinner.[58]

When Queen Victoria went to Switzerland she had with her, as might be expected of a nineteenth-century traveller, a Baedeker, that universal vade-mecum of her era, as well as other maps and books.[59] Wherever she was she continued her voluminous correspondence on writing paper headed with the royal cypher and stamped with the address of her hotel or villa. Her sitting room in Grasse contained all the familiar clutter of her sitting rooms at home: family photographs (Albert pre-eminent among them) crowded round the blotter on the writing table and lined the walls in ranks, and despatch boxes, writing paper and books all occupied the same positions as at home. No wonder she concluded her account in her journal of her arrival in the south of France: 'much unpacking!'[60] At Grasse she even had primroses sent out twice a week from the woods at Osborne.[61]

So far, so reasonable, one might say; but there was more. In 1845 her own travelling chaise took her part

On Villa Clara writing paper Queen Victoria asks her private secretary how much she could see during an excursion on Lake Maggiore.

of the way to Coburg. In 1862, when she was at Reinhardsbrunn for five weeks, she took her own horses abroad for the first time. Nine servants, twelve horses and four carriages were booked on the General Steam Company's vessel *Dolphin*, bound for Antwerp on 21 August 1862.[62] Horses, men and carriages, in the charge of Mr Wagland, the Queen's coachman, went on by train. They rested overnight on the 23rd at the Hotel Belle Vue in Cologne.[63] A week later one man and two ponies followed.[64] The Queen herself boarded the royal yacht at Greenhythe on 1 September and arrived at Reinhardsbrunn on 5 September (having paused to see Uncle Leopold in Belgium), where she was met by her own carriage, the horses having had plenty of time to recover from their journey by the time they were needed. Presumably, however, twelve horses and two ponies were not enough because when she went to Germany the following year the same number of men and carriages, together with seventeen horses, made the crossing.[65]

Her own horses did not always go abroad. Sometimes it was only her carriage: her 'own dear Scotch sociable',[66] still kept today in the Royal Mews,

The Illustrated London News showed its readers the scene of the Queen's arrival at Grasse: 'I was most kindly received with all honours', she wrote on 24 March 1891. 'The hotel is half a mile from the station, and I drove in my own landau, and my own horses . . . The little streets were crowded with enthusiastic people.'

bears a brass plaque recording the fact that it met her at the station on her trip to Switzerland in 1868. At Baveno in 1879 she arrived at the Villa Clara in her own waggonette, 'driven by Mr Henfrey's coachman, with Italian horses decorated with bells in regular Italian style'.[67] Hungarian horses which went 'wonderfully fast and quietly' took her back to the station when she left Baveno to return to England.[68] At Menton in 1882 she had an English coachman, with horses and outriders from Milan.[69]

An outrider always rode ahead of the carriage when the Queen drove out. His mount, complete with blinkers, matched the pair in harness so that if one of the horses in the Queen's carriage went lame it could be substituted. Driving the Queen was a great responsibility. Accidents to horse-drawn carriages were frequent, and even the famous Windsor greys were not immune to fright. At Grasse (where eight of them had preceded her arrival) a minor incident occurred as the Queen was passing a new military railway under construction near a beauty spot, and the blasting frightened them. While for afternoon drives she rode in style behind her superb coach horses, for her morning outing

Queen Victoria in her donkey carriage at Grasse, 1891. It was thus that the old Queen got about locally on the paths which had been specially widened and sanded for her use. Her youngest daughter, Princess Beatrice, or a lady-in-waiting would walk alongside.

when she did not go so far afield, the elderly Queen would take the air in a stout little carriage with thick rubber wheels which she called her garden chair. Between the shafts was a donkey, which in 1891 was described as 'plump as a well-fed monk'.[70] She had first come across her Savoyard ass, Jacquot, on a visit to Aix-les-Bains; he was thin and overworked and she bought him on the spot.

Furniture was sometimes sent ahead from England for the Queen's travels abroad. In 1890 she booked the entire Maison Mottet (renamed the Villa Victoria), the double annexe to the Hotel de l'Europe which she and her retinue took over in its entirety every time they came to Aix-les-Bains. *The New York Herald* informed its readers that a large pitch pine bed had been sent from Windsor, with canopy and curtains of white linen and 'remarkably fine' bed linen embroidered with the Queen's monogram. The rooms which the Queen was to occupy had been entirely redecorated; her salon had been furnished in crimson satin with Indian embroidery, and as 'a delicate attention', Monsieur Bernascon, the proprietor, had hung portraits of the Prince and Princess of Wales on the walls; in the dining room, which had been enlarged since her last visit in 1887, was an engraving of the Queen herself.

The 'delicate attention' was nothing so very new; on her first trip to Germany Queen Victoria noticed that 'In all the Inns, they had hung up our portraits . . . and at Frankfurt and Deutz they had mine with the two children, by Landseer'.[71] At Schloss Brühl on the same trip, as the guest of the King of Prussia, she found a portrait of the Prince of Wales by William Hansel, which the king, who was the child's godfather, had sent for specially from Berlin.[72]

Hotels were always redecorated prior to her arrival and often new roads were made – from the road into the Thüringer Wald in 1845, 'made by the poor people in *2* days'[73] so that she could attend a *battue*, to one in Grasse which was mended and sanded in order that she might drive along it in her garden chair. Gardens would be closed to the public for her, as at Aix-les-Bains in 1885, where she walked out in the garden of the Maison Mottet 'and in the adjoining one of the "Cercle", both of which are kept private for me, but are always open during the Season'.[74]

The music room at Schloss Brühl as it looked in 1845, when Queen Victoria stayed here as the guest of the King of Prussia. To the left of the fireplace is William Hansel's portrait of the infant Prince of Wales, hung specially for the Queen's visit. (Watercolour by A. Wegelin.)

New roads and wallpaper and somewhere private for Her Majesty to take the air were only part of the story. The host prince or hotel proprietor also had to provide servants. They were never few. When in 1862 the widow Queen and her children left Reinhardsbrunn, which belonged to her brother-in-law, Duke Ernst II of Coburg, no fewer than two hundred servants, lent by the duke for her visit, left too. Even the Queen must have thought this was remarkable, for she mentioned it in her journal. At Aix-les-Bains in 1890 Monsieur Bernascon provided seventy servants for the Queen and her entourage of forty-odd people at the Villa Victoria.

Unseen preparations also took place. At Grasse three extra telegraphic clerks were laid on, and the telegraph service was open day and night. As *The Times* of 31 March 1885 reassured those of its readers who might think that their sovereign was shirking her duty, before leaving England 'the Queen directed that arrangements should be made for keeping Her Majesty constantly informed by telegraph from her Ministers of all important proceedings'. Even in her very old age, sitting out in the gardens of the Villa Liserbe at Cimiez, the Queen still spent the morning working through her official boxes and writing telegrams to be ciphered to London.[75] Quiet surveillance was also laid on.

Getting There

The new technology allowed the Queen to travel and still stay in close touch with home, but it was above all the railways which gave Queen Victoria the freedom of Europe. When she first began travelling in the 1840s, rail travel was in its infancy. Her visit to Coburg in 1845 was made before the railway was built, and she admitted herself that the journey was quite an undertaking. She was away for a month, but took comfort in the thought that 'with the present and speedy communications . . . in case of anything happening (all which Please God is most unlikely) I could come back'.[76]

On 9 August 1845 Her Majesty prorogued Parliament, signed two copies of her will and spent the night on the royal yacht, which left Woolwich at 3.45 a.m. By 6.00 p.m. it had arrived at Antwerp. The royal party spent a second

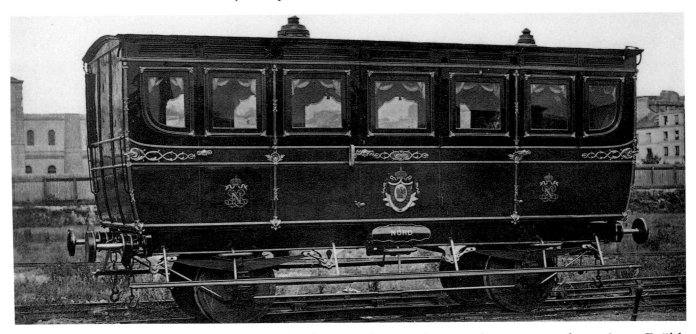

The royal saloon, in which Queen Victoria, Prince Albert, the Prince of Wales and the Princess Royal, accompanied by the Emperor Napoleon III, travelled from Boulogne to Paris in 1855. (Photograph by E. D. Baldus.)

night on board. The next day, 11 August, they went on by train to Brühl, between Cologne and Bonn. After two days as guests of the King of Prussia a Rhine steamer took them up the river from Bonn to Stolzenfels, just outside Koblenz, where they were due to spend one night but stayed for two. On 16 August they boarded their own boat, the *Fairy*, the tender to the royal yacht, which took them up the Rhine as far as Mainz, where they spent another two nights. East of the Rhine they took to the roads. At 7.00 a.m. on 18 August they got into their travelling chaise at Mainz; there followed two gruelling twelve-hour days in the chaise, changing horses every twenty miles or so. Sometimes the horses had been lent by a king, sometimes they were hired post horses. The royal party stopped at Würzburg, and eventually reached Coburg on 19 August, ten days after leaving England.

'We started at once in my new and very comfortable carriages, built at Brussels entirely on the plan of those I always use going to Scotland. viz. a sitting saloon, with compartment for attendants joining it, a little dressing room and bedroom, with compartment for maids adjoining the latter, all very prettily fitted up.'

28 MARCH 1876

It may seem a long, complicated journey, and would of course have been quicker without the visit to the King of Prussia, but Her Majesty had the benefit of the best that was available; ordinary travellers in Germany at this time could expect a German diligence to cover fifty-five miles in fourteen hours, an average of rather less than four miles an hour.

When the Queen and Prince Albert next went to Coburg in 1860 rail travel had entered a new era. They boarded the royal yacht on 22 September, spent the night on board, crossed the next day and spent that night on board at Antwerp; so far, no change from 1845. The next day, 24 September, they went on by train to Frankfurt where they spent the night, and on 25 September made the entire journey from Frankfurt to Coburg by train. The two twelve-hour, horse-drawn days had shrunk to eight hours by steam and the entire undertaking had been reduced from ten days to three. The rail journey was still complicated enough. They had to cross Mainz from one station to another in a brougham, and from Mainz to Frankfurt travelled in a railway carriage lent to them by the Grand Duke of Hesse-Darmstadt. From Frankfurt they went on in the King of Bavaria's railway carriage, which they kept all the way to Coburg, even though they changed onto a different railway company, the Thüringer Railway, at Lichtenfels.

As the years passed, travelling times continued to contract. In 1894, returning from Coburg, the Queen left at 6.45 p.m. and arrived at Windsor at 8.30 p.m. the following day. Three days had become less than twenty-six hours. Her journeys were very much speeded up when she began to travel overnight. Although it did save time and the expense of hotels, it was principally for reasons of comfort and convenience – it was much cooler for her – that the Queen took to travelling overnight. The first night that she spent on a foreign train was in 1862, her first journey without Albert.

She usually slept very well, and would arrive looking fresh and rested. One exception, perhaps, was when she went to Cannes in 1887: 'We have got a nice clean carriage', she wrote, 'with two coupés, one on either side, for the servants and maids . . . but nothing could have been more uncomfortable than my bed, very narrow, with too large a mattress squeezed in upon it.'[77] Usually the train would stop for less than five minutes at any station, occasionally for fifteen for Her Majesty to take coffee, or perhaps a little turn outside, but would halt for about an hour and twenty minutes to allow her to dine.

Queen Victoria always travelled by special train, even as the Countess of Balmoral, for whom the railway companies would create illuminated timetables as ornate as any medieval manuscript. It was no easy business

The royal yacht, the first *Victoria and Albert*, with the Queen on board, entering Ostend on 15 September 1843. (Watercolour by L. T. Francia.)

coordinating times. In 1879, the year she went to Baveno, there was a time difference of ten minutes between London and Paris. All Swiss railways ran by Berne time, which was twenty minutes ahead of Paris time, and all Italian railways by Roman time, forty-seven minutes ahead of Paris time.[78] When she went from Aix-les-Bains to Darmstadt in 1890 she left Aix and halted at Geneva on Paris time, left Geneva and arrived at Basel on Berne time, left Basel and arrived at Darmstadt on Karlsruhe time. Careful timing and meticulous planning could, however, be thrown into confusion by the elements, or indeed by the Queen, herself an elemental force: 'The Queen wishes it to be *understood* that she will *not start* if it *blows* hard tomorrow.'[79]

During Victoria's long reign the royal yacht was replaced several times. The first, when the Queen came to the throne, was an old sailing ship, the *Royal George*, which had been launched in 1817, two years before she was born. Queen Victoria and Prince Albert went to Scotland in her in 1842, rather ignominiously towed by two steam vessels. The Queen complained that the speed was too slow and so a paddle-steamer was hired for the return journey.

The following year a brand new steam yacht, the *Victoria and Albert*, was launched. This was the ship which took the royal couple to France and Belgium in 1843. For the trip to Germany in 1845 the interior was improved and some problems ironed out: the cabins were ventilated, the galleries between the paddleboxes widened and the interiors painted to imitate pale satinwood.[80]

A special timetable for a special train in the year of the Queen's Diamond Jubilee, 1897, when she travelled from Cherbourg to Nice as Madame la Comtesse de Balmoral.

Voyage de Madame la Comtesse de BALMORAL

Marche Route de

CHERBOURG à NICE

Stations	Heures d'arrivée	Temps d'arrêt	Heures de départ	Stations	Heures d'arrivée	Temps d'arrêt	Heures de départ
	h. m.	h. m.	h. m.		h. m.	h. m.	h. m.
Le Jeudi 11 Mars 1897					matin		matin
CHERBOURG Dép.	matin	—	10.25	Mâcon	2.21	3	2.24
Lison	midi 4	5	midi 9	Lyon	3.33	5	3.38
Caen	1.12	6	1.18	Valence	5.19	3	5.22
Lisieux	2.9	4	2.13	Avignon	7.12	55	8.7
Conches	3.19	4	3.23	Tarascon	8.30	1.15	9.45
Mantes	4.34	15	4.49	Marseille (Bifurcation de Toulon)	11.23	10	11.33
Noisy-le-Sec	5.58	15	6.13	Toulon	midi 45	5	midi 50
Villeneuve-St-Georges (Triage)	6.46	7	6.53	Les Arcs	2.5	5	2.10
Laroche	9.6	43	9.49	Cannes	3.7	5	3.12
Les Laumes	11.18	8	11.26	Nice Arr.	3.45	—	soir
Dijon	mün.21	5	mün.26	Le Vendredi 12 Mars 1897			

G. de Metz

Ed. Blount

Saloon on the second, and much larger, *Victoria and Albert*. The Queen found it all 'most comfortable' when she first used it, crossing to France in 1855. Weather permitting, she would sketch on deck, or would otherwise read and work in her sitting room or sometimes play piano duets with the children. (Watercolour by E. A. Penley, *c.*1864.)

Twelve years later a new royal yacht was launched. In March 1855 the Queen noted in her journal, 'Albert has been all over the new yacht, which he describes as magnificent.'[81] They tried her out on 11 July, when the Queen agreed that she was 'indeed a most magnificent and enormous vessel. One feels quite lost in her!'.[82] This new ship, also called *Victoria and Albert*, remained the Queen's principal yacht for the rest of her life. It was a very beautiful vessel, and fast, being capable of an average speed of 15.4 knots. Inside, as far as the royal apartments were concerned, it was a veritable floating palace, with a bedroom, dressing room and drawing room for the Queen, hung with chintz patterned with rosebuds and green silk and carpeted throughout. The woodwork was all bird's-eye maple and the door handles were of ivory.[83] The yacht was equipped with everything for the Queen's comfort that one could possibly imagine: there was a piano; there were little stoves of porcelain painted with flowers; and her drawing room was hung with charts and maps on spring-rollers (though later these seem to have been superseded by portraits of Prince Albert and other members of the family). She dined in a kind of 'pavilion' on deck, which had large plate glass windows, a painted porcelain stove and a coal scuttle in the shape of a nautilus shell, and along the white and gold cornice ran the motifs of Her Majesty's United Kingdom – the English rose, the Scottish thistle and the Irish shamrock. Besides accommodation for the Queen, there were spacious

Charabanc presented to Queen Victoria by King Louis-Philippe, similar to those they rode in together at Eu; 'We were very merry and laughed a good deal', wrote the Queen on 3 September 1843. (Watercolour; artist unknown.)

rooms for the royal children and generous cabins for the ladies, gentlemen and servants of the suite, and quarters for the crew of 240.[84] As with her palaces, where the furniture and decorations chosen by Albert were never changed, so with her yacht: for fifty years the Queen changed nothing until her eyesight began to fail, and she was persuaded to have electric lighting fitted; and very pretty she thought her cabin looked with it.

The captain of the royal yacht in 1876, who was also her nephew, had other cares besides his usual maritime duties. For instance, he had to remember Her Majesty's dislike of heated rooms. 'My dearest Aunt', he was writing to the Queen before she left for Baden-Baden, 'I will take care there are no stoves, either in your bedroom or in your sitting room cabins, only I am afraid you will find it very cold.' He went on to reassure her that 'the North East Wind which is blowing at present is a fair wind for Cherbourg and we may expect smooth water'.[85] In 1899, on her last trip to the south of France, Queen Victoria was persuaded that the journey would be easier for her if she crossed from Folkestone to Boulogne in the steamship *Calais-Douvre*. Every conceivable arrangement was made for her comfort: a special cabin was built on deck and equipped with furniture from the *Victoria and Albert*. On leaving Boulogne Her Majesty expressed satisfaction with the arrangements, but said she would make the return journey in her own yacht.[86]

The Honoured Hosts

Before the Queen left for home again she would be occupied with the ordering of 'endless' presents, which she considered 'de rigueur'.[87] She realized how much they meant to the recipients but it was a question which had to be approached with some delicacy. In 1860 gentlemen who had been of service to the Queen during her visit to Coburg were rewarded with snuff boxes, but 'subsequently requested to be allowed to return them for their value in money'.[88] When considering the question of presents two years later, the Keeper of the Privy Purse, Sir Charles Phipps, took into account not only that the snuff boxes had been sniffed at but also that in the Queen's widowhood a new order applied: 'Upon this occasion', he wrote, 'as the visit is a strictly private one, and all the expenses of every kind are paid by the Queen, no snuff boxes have been bought – a ring or pin might probably be given to the Baron. Should the Queen prefer it, snuff boxes could be easily got from London.'[89] Baron Griesheim, 'the person who has been most employed', received a bracelet for his wife.[90] The stable master at Reinhardsbrunn had also been in constant attendance and Sir Charles reminded Her Majesty that 'the horses are all the Queen's, and he has no control over them. Still he should have a present.'[91] She gave him a pin. The castellan received studs, the gardener a pencil case and the castellan's wife a brooch. On behalf of the Prince of Wales, the head forester received a pin. There were rings and pins for officials who had shown the royal children round places of interest, and pins and studs for the 'Railway Authorities', with a watch for the outrider, studs for the head cook, pins for the footmen, a brooch for a housemaid and a set of studs for Kanné. As usual, these presents were nicely graded to suit the status of the recipient.[92] And what about the clergymen who had officiated at the services for the Queen? They too, advised Sir Charles, should receive something besides the payment of their expenses. It was possible they might prefer a 'money present' and he took means '*delicately* to ascertain this'.[93]

The Privy Purse was careful in its expenditure: jewellery that was bought in Coburg in 1860 but not immediately given away would, said Sir Charles, 'be very useful upon future occasions. The English jewellery being much more expensive, and not making nearly so much show for the same money.'[94]

As well as jewellery the Queen gave representations of herself. A hotel proprietor in Cimiez received her two-foot-high bronze bust on a black plinth. During the little ceremony of presentation the bust rolled off its plinth and fell at her feet; Queen Victoria was much amused.[95]

Queen Victoria's coat of arms in stained glass. This and its pair, depicting Prince Albert's arms, were given by Queen Victoria to the King of Prussia in 1845 when she stayed at Stolzenfels, where they still hang today.

CHAPTER TWO

The Pilgrimage to Coburg, 1845

Schloss Brühl

Anyone who follows in Queen Victoria's footsteps had better be prepared for dizzy heights and extraordinary contrasts: one day in a splendid palace, the next hunting through village back gardens for a long-lost view. Her name crops up wherever she went. In a saracen stronghold at Gourdon outside Grasse, high among the mountains, remote, grand and wild, you come across a little blue nameplate screwed into the ancient stones: Place Victoria. The legacy she has left in these places is almost entirely one of great good will. Aix-les-Bains, today a quiet backwater, looks back on its *belle époque* with proud nostalgia; and it will be hard to forget the morning in a small village near the Rosenau when we were hunting down a view the Queen had once painted of a few half-timbered houses and a suggestion of hills that might be the distant Thüringer Wald. The previous day we had been at Würzburg, in many-splendoured halls; now we are in the house of a pair of village elders. The old lady is very deaf, but when she finally understands the purpose of our visit her old face expands into a brilliant smile, 'Ah!' she cries, 'Die Königen *Victoria*!'; she raises her hands and her old features light up like the blazing fireworks which celebrated the travels of the young, wide-eyed Queen.

We begin our journeys in the foreign country which was most important to Queen Victoria, Germany, where she went in 1845 to see the birthplace of her beloved Albert.

Modern Germany is fast, efficient, very high tech. Powerful cars race along the motorways where there are no speed limits, past the vast shining factories grinding out Germany's wealth. A metallic smell hangs in the air. Fields are flat and featureless. We are skirting Cologne, heading towards Bonn. It seems hard to imagine Queen Victoria here.

We start to pick up signs to Brühl: they kindle flickers of excitement for it is

Schloss Brühl, outside Cologne, as it is today. Here, in 1845, Queen Victoria spent her first night in Germany.

strange to see the name, familiar from faded handwriting in the Royal Archives, blazoned across a road sign. The town of Brühl itself, going about its daily business, offers no sense of the past, but, as we turn in between tall lime trees and the sun comes out, excitement turns to recognition. There on the left is the little station where Queen Victoria arrived from Cologne. It is now painted strawberry pink. A train pulls out, heading for Bonn.

We turn up the cobbled entrance to the palace, between menacing guardian figures on the sentry boxes and wide green lawns. In the moat below, huge grey carp float like ghosts, and a pair of swans with their seven cygnets glide slowly under the bridge, arching their white necks. And here we are, face to

The staircase at Schloss Brühl, even more overwhelming and dramatic than we had expected from the watercolour painted by A. Wegelin (right). This picture was among the set of paintings of the palace given to Queen Victoria by her host, King Frederick William IV of Prussia. The gilded bust of the Elector Clemens Auguste looks down at us. On the ceiling is a fresco by Carlo Carlone.

face with a building which Queen Victoria would have recognized instantly, glowing in the sunshine, painted yellow and grey, with statues blowing a fanfare from the rooftops on golden trumpets: Schloss Brühl.

The two great wings of the palace seem to stretch out their arms in welcome – and this unsettling fantasy intensifies when one of the row of clipped bay trees, standing to attention outside the door, gets up and moves away. Then, behind its tub, we see the gardeners carrying it off to its winter quarters out of the frost, and reality settles precariously back into place.

Standing in the central hall, however, where Queen Victoria's carriage drove right in and stopped at the foot of the stairs, we wonder again if we can believe what we see. The ethereal watercolours in the souvenir albums, breathtaking though they are, have not really prepared us for this.

Huge columns tower over us, painted and polished to look like marble, swirling with captured bubbles of colour, ochre and sea green. At the foot of the stairs stand groups of giant figures, laughing and gesticulating as if more

'Colossal marble statues, breathtaking in their grandeur and vitality, flank the staircase. I looked up from where I was standing, close to the spot where Queen Victoria's carriage once halted, and gazed at this masterpiece of fantasy. The schloss is still used for state entertaining by the German government, and has been visited on several occasions by Queen Victoria's great-great-granddaughter, Her Majesty Queen Elizabeth II.'

interested in us than in holding up the enormous staircase that they so carelessly support, which seems to leap up into space as it divides above them. Over our heads a leafy chandelier is suspended from a distant frescoed ceiling round the edge of which, in a flurry of virtuoso plasterwork, are pairs of muscular giants which still have enough energy left, after supporting the ceiling for more than two hundred years, to gossip and argue amongst themselves.

We set foot on the bottom step, feeling rather small, even alarmed, as the enormous staircase with its polished columns and writhing bodies seems to spring out at us. This is the work of a master hand, Balthasar Neumann, one of the finest exponents of the German Baroque, who specialized in creating a sense of vast scale.

High on the wall above the turn of the stair, between gleaming pink columns, we see – just as Queen Victoria might have done as she alighted from her carriage – a gilded bust surrounded by figures representing Magnanimity and Magnificence, Generosity and the Arts. She might also have seen, had she not been greeting the entire Prussian court who were waiting in state to welcome her, Reason and Virtue hurling Vice into the Abyss. It is all heady stuff, designed to impress, and to glorify the man who was responsible for all this – the original of the gilded bust – the Archbishop-Elector of Cologne, Clemens Auguste.

Born in 1700, he was a prince of the House of Wittelsbach. He became a Catholic bishop at the age of nineteen, but his palace suggests that he was a priest who preferred a morning's hawking, or a minuet with a pretty woman, to a *missa solemnis*. On our way in we had passed portraits of him as a dapper young man dressed for the hunt with a hawk on his wrist, and, later, looking regal as befitted a prince of the Church, swathed in scarlet silk and ermine.

His career in the Church brought him great revenues, power and prestige; but his passion was falconry, and in 1725 he laid the cornerstone of this splendid new hunting lodge on the site of a medieval fortress, some eight miles south-west of Cologne.

He employed the best architects, artists and landscape gardeners, but His Grace the Archbishop was a connoisseur and patron of more than just the fine arts. At one point there was a pause in his brilliant career when the Pope called him to Rome to account for the presence at his court of several particularly lovely Italian singers – though the pontiff doesn't appear to have objected to the court dwarf, the court fool and the one hundred and fifty court chamberlains that Clemens Auguste also maintained.

It took forty-five years to complete the work on the palace which was not finished until 1768, seven years after Clemens Auguste, dying as he had lived, had danced himself to death in a minuet.

Barely a generation later, in 1794, the palace was occupied by French Revolutionary troops, and when Napoleon, who was accustomed to take whatever he liked from those he had defeated, saw Schloss Brühl, he is supposed to have remarked that it was a pity it was not on wheels. Since he couldn't take it with him, he gave it to Marshal Davoust, who let it fall into disrepair. When the Napoleonic upheavals subsided the palace became the property of the kings of Prussia, and it was King Frederick William IV of Prussia who was Queen Victoria's host there.

11 August 1845 had been a very long day for the English Queen. She and her German husband had been up since 5.30 a.m. Having left the royal yacht at Flushing, they had slowly traversed her Uncle Leopold's realm of Belgium in his royal train and had been welcomed into German territory at Aix-la-Chapelle (or Aachen). There the Queen had stopped to see, amongst other wonders, the skull of Charlemagne. The silver and gold reliquary in which it is kept is made in the shape of his head and shoulders, and studded with little black

The dining, or music room, at Schloss Brühl. (Watercolour by A. Wegelin.) You can also see a train arriving at the station, just visible through the window on the left.) BELOW: the arrival of Her Majesty at the station, as depicted by *The Illustrated London News*.

imperial eagles and precious stones the size of wine gums; his arm and thigh bones are encased in gold of marvellous workmanship. She had been greeted by kings, princes, bürgermeisters and deputations of maidens dressed in white, and when she drove through Cologne from one railway station to another they had sprinkled the streets with eau-de-Cologne.

It was dark when she reached Brühl, at the end of a long, tiring journey, and her ladies-in-waiting were 'almost blind and deaf with fatigue',[1] but the Queen herself was still alert, observant and fascinated by the people she was meeting. The king, she commented, 'is grown fatter, but is as amusing as ever; his temper is violent, and he scolds his servants amazingly'.[2] She

eyed his wife sympathetically. At forty-four, Queen Elisabeth's chances of producing an heir to the Prussian throne were almost gone: 'The Queen has no remains of good looks – her features were never regular – but she had beautiful eyes; her eyelids however are very red now, and she looks so haggard and suffering and pale. She is not *very* tall, and is lame, but she conceals it very gracefully . . . she is very kind and natural but not very demonstrative, and she looks unhappy & suffering, but their Ménage is as happy as possible.'[3]

Queen Victoria was shown upstairs (the great staircase, unlike anything in England, must have seemed quite extraordinary). As we follow her route up the marble steps, the Hall of the Guards at the top of the stairs looks just like its watercolour, all green and yellow, painted to imitate marble, and on the ceiling is a throng of frescoed gods paying homage to a distinguished relation of Clemens Auguste. Beyond is the dining and music room, pink and white and grey, frothy with plasterwork; a gallery runs round the walls so that people could watch when the Elector gave a public dinner. How empty these rooms

'To hear the people speaking German and to see German soldiers, seemed strange. I overheard people saying that I looked "sehr Englisch"'.

11 AUGUST 1845

The unveiling of the statue of Beethoven in Bonn, in the presence of the King of Prussia and the Queen of England. Her Majesty's visit coincided by chance with the first Beethoven festival.

seem, with their shining expanses of parquet, when you have peopled them in your mind's eye with visiting sovereigns.

From these windows Queen Victoria looked down onto the palace forecourt (where we had seen the trees on the move) and listened to six hundred musicians, from the bands of thirty Prussian regiments, playing a *Zapfenstreich*, or tattoo, the entire scene illuminated by lamps of coloured glass; 'the whole was the finest thing I ever heard',[4] she wrote. She thought that she had never heard 'God Save the Queen' played better; even the rather supercilious correspondent of *The Illustrated London News* conceded that this 'monster Band' played to perfection.

At last she was able to write: 'We retired to our rooms, they are 4 – looking to the garden with beautiful ceilings, gilt and painted; & pictures of the Electors of Cologne.'[5]

You can still identify the four rooms she meant, but to do so you have to look quite hard into corners of the ceilings, which are painted with hunting motifs, herons, saucy pastoral scenes and monkeys practising falconry. When Queen Victoria was here the palace had been newly decorated by her host, a genial, hasty monarch with a bent for architecture. By the 1840s the palace's rococo style was regarded as fusty and old-fashioned, and Frederick William IV, like most of the rest of Germany, was on a Gothic Revival spree. The Elector's elegant walls were hung with violent red and green curtains, and outsize gothic chairs with red plush seats and monstrous, heavy tables were introduced. Their scale would have dwarfed the tiny Queen. Today this furniture has been consigned in some embarrassment to a large empty room at the back of the palace, the virulent draperies have been swept away, and the rooms have been returned to their soft, eighteenth-century colour schemes of biscuit and eau-de-Nil, apple green and dusty pink, and are being gradually furnished with eighteenth-century pieces.

Still, it is easy to imagine in these sunny, peaceful rooms what a lovely place it must have been for Victoria and Albert to come back to and rest at intervals during the busy programme of entertainments which King Frederick William had prepared for them in nearby Cologne and Bonn.

Queen Victoria's visit to the King of Prussia is chiefly remembered for the ceremonial unveiling of the statue of Beethoven in Bonn on 12 August 1845, during the first Beethoven festival. No one, however, had thought through properly the arrangements for the ceremony, and when the statue was uncovered it had its back to the balcony where the royal party stood, which 'had the most absurd effect of rudeness on his part'.[6] The statue still stands in the same place, in the middle of the market square opposite the Post Office, looking every inch the figure of a truculent genius.

Bonn still blushes at its *faux pas*, and most summers will bring a newspaper article referring to it, but Queen Victoria thoroughly enjoyed her visit, for the rest of the morning was taken up with visiting her husband's student haunts,

The house where Prince Albert lived while a student at the University of Bonn. (Watercolour by C. Höhe.) 'It was such a pleasure to me to be able to see this house,' wrote the Queen on 14 August 1845, 'we went all over it, and it is *just* as it was – in *no way* altered.' Sadly, it was not possible for us to follow the Queen into this period of her husband's past as the house no longer exists.

meeting the professors about whom he had told her so many stories, and seeing the little house overlooking the minster where he had lived. It was still exactly the same, she was glad to see, down to 'the very sofa on which my dearest Albert lay when he had his bad leg'.[7]

That evening they took the train from Brühl into Cologne to see the illuminations from a boat on the river; 'anything more beautiful cannot be imagined', wrote the Queen, 'blue and red lights – Rockets – salutes of every kind and sort. Houses, illuminated so as to appear red hot – & finally the Cathedral glowing red – the most splendid thing possible, and all that reflected in that splendid river, the Rhine.'[8]

The following morning she attended a concert in Bonn, part of the celebrations for the Beethoven festival, but lamented that there was not enough Beethoven played. In the afternoon (her programme was as packed as a royal programme of today) she went to see the work in progress on Cologne Cathedral, which had stood unfinished for six hundred years. Work began on it in 1248, and was abandoned in 1509. When Dorothy Wordsworth saw its

Schloss Brühl from the gardens, where the fountains were turned on specially for us.

unfinished and ruinous state in 1820, she spoke for her generation when she described it as 'an everlasting monument of riches and grandeur, and I fear of devotion passed away: of sublime designs unaccomplished – remaining, though not wholly developed, sufficient to incite and guide the dullest intellect'.[9] In 1830, however, the original plans for the cathedral were discovered and, this coinciding with the flush of gothic enthusiasm, work on the great building recommenced in 1842, to be completed finally in 1880. The cathedral miraculously escaped too much damage during the Second World War, and today its dark, gothic silhouette dominates the silvery, cubic skyline of Cologne.

After admiring what there was of the cathedral, Victoria and Albert returned to Schloss Brühl for a 'family dinner' of twenty in the salon, and a concert of celebrities at which Jenny Lind, the 'Swedish nightingale', sang, Liszt played and Meyerbeer, foremost operatic composer of the day, accompanied his own compositions.

As we stand at the tall state apartment windows overlooking the gardens, thinking about the bustle and gaiety of 1845, the fountains in the circular pools

The garden façade in the 1840s. Victoria and Albert's apartments, newly decorated, overlooked the gardens which were planted out in contemporary taste. Today, inside and outside, the palace has been restored to its eighteenth-century appearance. (Watercolour by A. Wegelin.)

below us suddenly spring into life, kindly turned on specially for us. Jets of water soar high into the air above the little box hedges that curl round flowerbeds splashed with red, yellow and blue in patterns like the embroidered cuffs on a dandy's sleeve. Pale gravel paths run between long, straight lines of clipped, shady, lime walks and the horizon is bounded by the tall trees of the deer park. No sign of the twentieth century is visible from these windows, unless you count the mechanical hedge clipper munching its way giraffe-like along the left-hand lime walk.

On the other hand, this was not quite the view that Queen Victoria would have seen. The Elector's garden, the work of the famous garden architect Dominique Girard, had, like the palace, fallen into disrepair under the Napoleonic occupation. In 1842 Frederick William had commissioned a worthy successor, Peter Joseph Lenné, one of the foremost landscape architects of his day, to renovate it, which he did most sensitively in the park but (to modern taste) less successfully in the gardens. Their swirling rococo patterns were out of fashion in the 1840s and he replaced them with the rather untidy arrangements that can be seen in the watercolour of the garden front.

The dining room in the summer apartments. The Queen's ladies-in-waiting had never seen anything like it before. Everything is designed to keep you as cool as possible, with marble floors, blue and white Dutch tiles on the walls and light, graceful furniture.

After the First World War Brühl came under the administration of state palaces and gardens in Berlin, and in the 1930s Girard's plans for the parterres were reconstructed so that, like the interiors, the garden now looks more like its eighteenth-century self than it did in 1845.

We leave the state rooms and return to the ground floor, where we find ourselves almost in another climate: whereas the upper rooms are warm and sumptuous, downstairs in the summer apartments the decorations are deliberately fresh and cool, the walls lined with blue and white Dutch tiles. In the dining room tables and chairs are painted white and their graceful legs are tipped with little black cloven hooves. In the corner a marble basin with running water serves as a wine-cooler. Chandeliers of milky glass hang like seaweed above marble floors. It is all less grand and less intimidating than the state rooms. Again there is a little thrill as we come in, for here are rooms already familiar from the account of Queen Victoria's journey written by one of her ladies-in-waiting, Lady Canning: 'The household breakfast was at 9 – quite English fashion – good tea and bread and butter and rolls. We had it in a room lined with Dutch tiles of large blue and white patterns unlike anything I ever saw.'[10]

As we leave the summer apartments we pass another painting of the Archbishop-Elector Clemens Auguste, at a fancy-dress ball in Bonn, among masked gallants and their fair mistresses. In the background of the painting, not far from the Elector, is a curious figure, half-male and half-female, reputed to be Casanova: a far cry from the respectable, *gemütlich* world inhabited by Victoria and Albert, a world that did not survive for long at Brühl because it did not belong in this rococo fantasy.

We count ourselves lucky that we can still see the rooms where Queen Victoria stayed and the garden on which she looked out: it was all so nearly lost when it was hit by allied bombs during the Second World War, and several fine rooms were destroyed. Today the damage is invisible, but the curators still wage war on the effects of time, and the work of restoration is never-ending, from the re-carving of the statues on the rooftops to the gilding on the shutters.

It is interesting to learn that some of the materials in the palace have been woven from patterns in the Victoria and Albert Museum. This discovery gives us a sense of circular benefits: we came looking for Queen Victoria, who had been brought here by Albert, only to discover that the foundation which they created in London is helping to further the conservation of the place where she spent her first night on German soil.

Today Schloss Brühl is known as Augustusburg, and is a working palace. It belongs to the state of North-Rhine-Westphalia, is open to the public and is used for official entertaining. Queen Elizabeth II has been here three times on state visits, in 1965, in 1978, and just two days before we arrived; the yellow awnings are still up, and we have a sort of double vision, with recent televised images of her visit superimposing themselves on that of Queen Victoria. Her Majesty the Queen gave the president of Germany a handsomely bound volume containing reproductions of the watercolours which King Frederick William had given her great-great-grandmother nearly one hundred and fifty years before, with transcriptions of Queen Victoria's journal describing her visit. At the end of our own day there one comment of Queen Victoria's seems all too understandable: 'I have seen so many things that I am *quite* bewildered.'[11]

The Castle of Stolzenfels

When Queen Victoria and Prince Albert left Schloss Brühl they took a train to the railway station in Bonn and a carriage to the bank of the Rhine, where they embarked on the next stage of their long journey to the land of Albert's birth.

It was a very well planned trip. The royal couple had come as far as they could by the most modern and comfortable means but the railways went no further; now they were going to enjoy, from the deck of a paddle-steamer, the fashionably wild and romantic scenery of the most spectacular stretch of the Rhine.

One of the first landmarks they passed as they left Bonn was a towering crag, to Queen Victoria, 'that beautiful, steep, commanding Drachenfels',[12] the scene of an episode in one of the great legends which the powerful waters of this river have gathered around themselves. Here the mythical hero Siegfried was supposed to have killed the dragon that haunted the rock, and to have bathed in its blood so that he became invincible (though he had one weak spot where a linden leaf had fluttered down and landed between his shoulder blades). Victoria thrilled to it all: 'On the Drachenfels Siegfried killed the dragon. *Too* beautiful.'[13] That she was swept away by the romance of the great river is not surprising: the Rhine has a powerful presence as it hurries past you down to the sea.

Very shortly Queen Victoria set eyes on the first vineyards she had ever seen. She was delighted with the landscape, and in many ways her description of it still holds good today:

At every turn of this most beautiful and unique river the Rhine you have another beautiful view, – and so many villages with those curious wooden houses and little spiral churches so indescribably picturesque – all the people out – and all the little schools drawn up – and the bells ringing, – here and there a crucifix or Madonna, in a vineyard, and on the top of one of the mountains a cross.[14]

She could not admire it in peace, however, for all the little towns and villages wanted to pay their respects with bells and cannonfire, until the Queen protested that 'The firing everywhere, from all the steamboats & in all the little villages was beyond everything and quite tiring'[15], while at Koblenz 'it was like a battle'.[16]

Queen Victoria passing the Drachenfels on her way up the Rhine in the *Fairy*, the tender to the royal yacht.

Romantic Stolzenfels as it looked when the Queen stayed here. She called it a '*Bijou* of a castle', and liked it so much that she spent an extra night. (Watercolour by G. Osterwald.)

Queen Victoria and Prince Albert's immediate destination was Stolzenfels, and so was ours.

This is a mustard yellow castle nestling in the woods high on the steep west bank of the Rhine, just south of Koblenz. You see it from a distance, looking noble, and then you lose sight of it as you drive along the riverside and slow down into the nondescript village of Kappellan.

We turn into a most unpromising entrance, squeeze through a narrow gate, and suddenly find ourselves in the shadow of the overhanging woods, climbing a steep, winding track, between high, forbidding walls. Ivy crawls over the stones, and we wouldn't be surprised to see bats come twittering out of the gloom. We take a deep breath and press on. The road passes under a massive archway and then snakes round so that we cross over the route we have come. The ascent is steep and slippery. Halfway up it a stream cascades down.

We wind on up the hill, the woods around us flaming with autumn colours,

gold and russet, and pass by some very grand buildings which we think at first are the castle but which turn out to be its stables, with the date 1843 above the gate. Finally we emerge from the wood.

In front of us a drawbridge spans a little valley, on the other side of which looms a cluster of yellow parapets and battlements clinging to a rocky outcrop. Beyond and far below glitters the Rhine. We cross the bridge, slip under the portcullis, through two archways, and stop in amazement.

We are in a narrow courtyard where tall yellow walls seem to be standing on tiptoe to peer down at us from their windows five storeys up. High on the tallest tower of all, sharp against the narrow rectangle of blue sky visible above the enclosing parapets, flies a long floating banner. Rapunzel herself might almost be behind one of these windows, startled by the witch as she waits for her Prince. 'Rapunzel, Rapunzel, let down your golden hair!' we call, but there is only the caretaker's wife behind a gauzy net curtain, watering her pink geraniums and taking no notice.

The effect is highly theatrical, and in its way stage-set medieval Stolzenfels is as much an escapist fantasy as Brühl. The castle does, however, have authentic medieval origins. It was built in the thirteenth century, and, like most of the

As we stand on the
terrace where
G. Osterwald painted this
view, it seems for a
moment that only the
distant river traffic has
changed since the day
Queen Victoria 'walked
out for a moment' with
Prince Albert to admire
the fountain and the
eagle.

castles for which the Rhine is famous, its purpose was the collection of tolls from the traffic plying the rich trading route below. Stolzenfels was eventually burnt down by the French in 1688, and was used as a quarry in the classically-minded eighteenth century, when ruins were interesting only if they had columns. In 1823, at just about the time when Germany was rediscovering the Middle Ages, Stolzenfels was given to the prince we have already met as Queen Victoria's host at Brühl, one of the most enthusiastic of romantics, then Crown Prince of Prussia. After he became Frederick William IV he had the castle rebuilt to plans by Karl Friedrich Schinkel, that illustrious architect who was perhaps best known for his mastery of the classical style but was well able later in life to design for the latest craze. In 1842 the king ceremonially entered his new castle with a large entourage, all in 'old German' dress.

Slender arches at the far end of the courtyard invite the eye through and down to a garden on a lower level, but first we want to see indoors. Up the steps to the pointed gothic door, turn left – and there we are, right inside one of the Royal Library watercolours. Here are the painted spandrels, the red plush chairs along the walls, the collection of glass and the rows of rare stoneware, all just as they were in the 1840s. On the walls we recognize the weaponry –

In the Queen's drawing room, apart from the missing carpet, and the murals which were not yet finished when C. Graeb painted this watercolour, past and present become almost indistinguishable.

muskets, crossbows, lances, breastplates – arranged in the same patterns as they were in 1845, though one or two pieces are now missing. In the middle of the room rise two most inconvenient black pillars, around which the specially constructed dining table used to stand. Here we are in what Queen Victoria called the 'very pretty sort of Hall, ornamented with armour'[17] where Frederick William entertained her, and where she listened one evening to a concert given by Madame Viardot, Pischek, Meyerbeer and Jenny Lind.

And here, across the way, is the room that, according to the Queen, 'they call the painted room'. Below gothic archways painted with idealized scenes of knightly virtue, Victoria was treated to tea by the faded, childless Queen of Prussia: 'quite in the German way; we Princesses sat down to a table, where there was no cloth, and dicke Milch [soured milk] and excellent cakes and Kirschkuchen [cherry cakes] were served. – The Queen's Ladies making the tea.'[18]

A narrow, winding staircase – this, too, is familiar from the souvenir albums, and now it is such fun to find out where it leads – takes us up to the main rooms above. The shining parquet creaks, a door swings back, and suddenly we step into a picture a hundred and fifty years old. Queen Victoria had been in raptures over these rooms: 'Our apartments (the Queen's) were quite lovely and so beautifully furnished. The sitting room has two turrets to it, *besides* the other two windows – which make little rooms of themselves with curtains to draw ... The room is exquisitely furnished, with beautiful tables and furniture, and carved things in wood, & painted glass round the windows.'[19]

It is a room to linger in and marvel at: the sofas and chairs are covered in extraordinarily rich silk brocatelle, whose exquisite design (gothic, of course) in russet, violet blue and gold is just the colours of the woods outside. The writing desk in one of the turrets, the green clock, even the octagonal table,

Lady Canning's sketch of
the view from
Stolzenfels, towards
Lahneck. 'Lady Canning
has been sketching
delightfully', remarked
the Queen on 15 August
1845.

inlaid with knights fluttering their pennants of mother-of-pearl through brassy woods as they gallop off to impossible deeds of derring-do – *it is all still here.*

It is a very intimate room. Framed by the cosy panelling is a vast fireplace lined with blue and white tiles. Little carved angels pray in the corners of the door frames, and in quiet, out-of-the-way alcoves the broad light of day is coloured and changed by the painted glass borders round the windows. You can almost smell the rich atmosphere, and perhaps if you were to pause here and sit quite still for a moment or two, letting the sounds of the busy world outside fall away, you might just hear the rustle of a silk skirt, the swish of lace and the scratch of pen on paper as the Queen's long, vigorous handwriting covers page after page of her journal with excited descriptions of everything she has seen and done.

'Arrived here in this *Bijou* of a castle, situated in the most beautiful position imaginable, looking *now* as I do, on that glorious beautiful Rhine, with which I am quite enchanted, so that I could sing "Mein Herz ist am Rhein" – I take up my description of Bonn.'[20] Later she looked out of the window again and confirmed that 'The views are quite too beautiful, you see on one side Coblence [Koblenz] and Ehrenbreitstein to the left, with Lahnstein in front of it; and on the other the ruin of Lahneck, Oberlahnstein, & the mountains which quite close in the Rhine, which is like a lake before you.'[21]

Perhaps she would break off to ask Albert the name of such and such a place, or to laugh with him at some little incident. How important it is to have the right travelling companion – to set the tone of the journey. How lucky Queen Victoria was to be seeing Germany through Albert's eyes, and to be reliving the experiences of his youth with him made her feel that she was not visiting a foreign country but coming home.

Beyond the Queen's drawing room is a narrow little passage which Victoria used as a dressing room. It is all much as her journal described: 'down three steps to our bedroom, also not large', furnished with a pretty, gothic bed on which there is still that curious arrangement of mattresses and pillows which foreign travellers to Germany used to complain about so bitterly, and which

The Queen's bedroom, which looks out over the garden.

left the sleeper 'half upright and sleepless in a sort of hammock shape'. Queen Victoria, hardy soul, 'slept exceedingly well and got up late'.[22]

Almost the whole of one wall of the bedroom is taken up by the window, where two large stained-glass roundels hang, one rich with Queen Victoria's coat of arms, the other with Albert's. They were presented to the King of Prussia on the occasion of this visit. Through the window we look down again on that magical garden, where a fountain plays among flowerbeds shaped, inevitably, like little pointed gothic arches.

We leave the bedroom and find ourselves in the King's apartments. Here it is all red plush and heavily carved sixteenth- and seventeenth-century cabinets, as masculine as the Queen's apartments are feminine. Once again we have stepped into one of the Royal Library watercolours, but this time there is a significant difference.

On the walls of the King's drawing room today hang four portraits which belong very decidedly to the nineteenth century. First, there is the handsome, round face of Frederick William IV, with a hint of red in his hair, whose company Queen Victoria enjoyed: 'We breakfasted very comfortably with the King and Queen, who are most amiable people, and so touchingly fond of each other; (I have seen them kiss one another, like [a] young married couple, and the Queen calls him "Liebchen" and the King is so amusing and so witty.)'[23]

Sadly, love could not bring children, and the King of Prussia was succeeded by his brother William I, who flares his muttonchop whiskers in the next portrait. As a result of the manoeuvrings of the Iron Chancellor, Bismarck, William became the head of a new, united Germany, and was declared German Emperor in 1871. Over in the far corner, with a manly blond beard flowing down his chest, is his son, Frederick III, who married Queen Victoria's eldest daughter. He was Germany's hope for a liberal monarchy, but when he succeeded his father he was a dying man, and three months later his son, William II, Queen Victoria's eldest grandchild, came to power. He is in the far corner by the window, with his fly-away moustachios. Their story ends in the First World War.

We retrace our steps down the narrow, winding stair, and at last go out into the garden. It has a Moorish feel, which comes as a bit of a surprise, but then this was a summer palace, and the garden is designed to make you feel cool on a hot day, with its trickling fountain, shady beds of ferns and vine-covered trellis. Deep in the wall is 'a seat overlooking the Rhine which is so pretty'.[24] Overhanging it are huge rose trees with thorns as big as spurs and heavy, blood-red blooms. Surrounded by hydrangeas stands a statue of the young Siegfried. He is supposed to be holding up his newly-forged sword, but seems to have mislaid it.

Queen Victoria took a turn here with her dearest Albert, and went out onto the terrace below her apartments, where she saw 'another beautiful fountain, surmounted by an eagle'. It is still there, but showing spots of rust through its gold plating.

Stolzenfels is full of the atmosphere of Queen Victoria, as Brühl had not been; it is wonderful to find it all so complete, and so redolent of the spirit of her time. She liked it so much that she decided to stay an extra night.

Chilled by the interiors, we lean over the terrace parapet, whose stones have been warmed by the sun. On the river far below, heavily laden barges come

sweeping downstream or labour up the other way. Some are stopping to unload at the depot on the far side. River police in a tiny green and white launch cross between them, and a sleek white pleasure steamer cruises by. Cars hurry along the roads that flank the river, a train rushes along the track on the far bank and a helicopter hovers overhead: we are being pulled back into the modern world, the industrial age, far from Queen Victoria and the tales of Siegfried killing the dragon.

We are hungry. Before leaving Stolzenfels we eat in the small café at the foot of the castle drive, with merry oom-pa-pa music pumping away in the background. A couple shaped like dumplings bring us wine and steaming tureens of delicious vegetable soup with floppy pink sausages, which send us into a comfortable stupor.

We spend the night in one of the places which Queen Victoria noticed: 'the pretty little town of Bopart [Boppard] with fine churches'.[25] The Rheinvilla, white art nouveau, set back from the promenade, is quiet and friendly. We sleep under the softest of feather duvets while the trains, no louder than a breeze through a wood, rush past on their way to Basel and the south. In the morning white pleasure boats put in at one of the floating docks just below the hotel windows, their gleaming superstructure half-seen through the golden leaves of the vine on the trellis that shades the terrace in summer.

ABOVE: 'From the moment of setting out I feel the excitement that surrounds every phase of our journey of discovery.'
OPPOSITE: In the shady garden Siegfried should be brandishing his newly forged sword but the blade is missing.

The Journey from the Rhine

When Queen Victoria came down to the embarkation point below Stolzenfels she found the tender to her own royal yacht waiting for her there. The *Fairy*, being screw-driven, boasted the very latest in maritime technology, and in this superior vessel, which (according to English reports, at least) caused a sensation on the Rhine, quickly outstripping the local paddle-steamers, the Queen set out to navigate the most dangerous and most spectacular stretch of the river.

On the deck of a Rhine pleasure boat you hear only the wind, the chuckle of the mighty river under the prow and the steady thrum of the engine. It is a wonderfully peaceful, leisurely way to travel. You escape the roads and the railways as they run cheek by jowl along each bank – a proximity deplored by Queen Victoria when years later she returned to the Rhine, as the trains would frighten horsedrawn traffic.

The cruiser pushes upstream about as fast as a cyclist on the bank. The wind comes from every direction, caught between the hills, some of whose rounded slopes are covered in vines growing in straight lines down the steep contours, others in woods now turning to gold.

In soft sunlight the water shimmers, and the hillsides soften to hazy blues, fading one beyond another, and the castles on their crags are shadowy silhouettes. How menacing they must once have been, controlled by robber barons who trained their cannon on the boatmen trying to navigate the treacherous waters below.

Queen Victoria recorded all the landmarks she passed, in particular the famous rocks of the Lorelei, 'which are extremely steep and fine, . . . where there is a peculiar echo; – this stream is extremely rapid and full of whirlpools and eddies'.[26] Here seductive water nymphs were supposed to lure unwary sailors to their deaths, and today, even though the reefs, which accounted for more lives than did any heartless nymphs, have been dynamited, the river still has to squeeze through the narrowest of gaps in the hills. Eddies swirl by, raising little snaking white curlicues on the thick green surface. The captain of the *Fairy* must have had a pilot to guide him through these treacherous reaches.

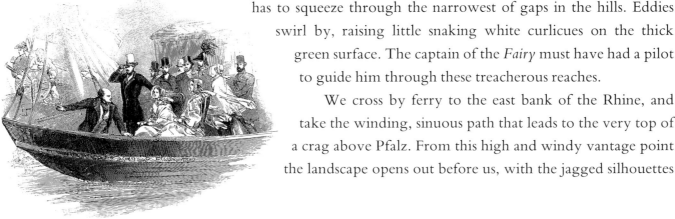

We cross by ferry to the east bank of the Rhine, and take the winding, sinuous path that leads to the very top of a crag above Pfalz. From this high and windy vantage point the landscape opens out before us, with the jagged silhouettes

Koblenz and the fortress of Ehrenbreitstein, by C. Scheuren. The Queen sat on the deck of the *Fairy* and eagerly took in all the sights she passed. Everywhere she was welcomed with decorations, bells and celebratory cannon fire.

of trees crowning the hilltops and the powerful river itself muscling its way through the valley far below.

Strange, overlapping slabs of grey slate protrude from this rocky outcrop, and to the right stands an ancient ruined tower, massive and silent, surveying the panorama through two lifeless windows. Its parapets have been overtaken by nature, but the hillsides below, stripped of their natural vegetation, have been ordered into neat rows of vines that now cover the slopes to the water's edge. This is the most dramatic stretch of the Rhine.

The Queen stayed up on deck for the best of the scenery, and at Bingen, where the landscape flattens out, she went below.

Mainz, where Victoria and Albert stopped for the night, we expect to look like the charming little watercolour from the Royal Library; instead we see square factory blocks, chimney stacks and two huge, matt black egg-shaped structures as big as gasworks. But even so the hazy sun and the distance lend enchantment. Queen Victoria recounts how when she arrived here she was greeted by an escort of Austrian and Prussian troops, a reminder that in 1845

'High on a crag above the Rhine, this was a quiet moment of meditation for me, when the spell of Queen Victoria yielded to the elemental·forces of wind, sun and river. Mountains always give me a deep sense of well–being, and here I drew strength and reassurance from the solid rock. The sunlight, which seemed pure and loving, poured over me and filled me with the warmth and hope of life, while the river flowed on like destiny. I felt very close to understanding the inner heart of things on that rock. I continued my journey more certain than ever that we must follow where the river of destiny takes us.'

Mainz, where the Queen spent the night. With this charming watercolour by H. Schilbach in our minds, we were unprepared for the modern city. We whizzed by on the motorway and swept onwards to Coburg.

Germany was still a loose affiliation of independent states, not yet a unified country. She slept at the Hotel de l'Europe, 'a very nice hotel', though she complained that 'the noise was very great in the streets'.[27]

The next day being Sunday they rested, and continued their journey at 7 o'clock on Monday morning in their travelling post chaise. 'The Post amused me much,' wrote the Queen, 'the horses all without winkers & the leaders being driven by the Postillion who rides the wheel horse, & his dress so peculiar. We came very well the whole day.'[28]

The Queen could be thankful she was spared the ordeal of ordinary travellers on the mail coaches, which averaged three miles an hour. The royal

post chaise bowled along through vineyards and orchards of apple, walnut and cherry. Everywhere crops were being harvested in the fields, and the Queen noted how hard the women worked, often barefoot and carrying heavy loads. She marked the changes in region as much by the differing shapes of the peasant women's caps as by the changes in the uniforms of her escort.

The post chaise changed horses every twenty miles or so, first at Hattersheim, where, since it was now in Hesse-Darmstadt territory, it acquired an escort of Hessian soldiers. One nineteenth-century traveller is reported to have become so frustrated by the constant border crossings with attendant customs (duty payable on such unlikely items as sugar plums), tolls, passports, backhanders and 'new coinage to puzzle his brains', that he simply threw all his money out of the carriage window.

Frankfurt, now a vast conurbation, was according to the Queen a 'really beautiful and very gay looking town'.[29] She liked the poplars she began to see

planted along the roads. Soon after the next change of horses, which was at Seligenstadt, they crossed the Bavarian frontier, so were now escorted by Bavarians ('The Postillions all through Bavaria wear light blue and a hat with feathers'),[30] and stopped at Aschaffenburg.

We glimpse Aschaffenburg from the autobahn, four tall domes in the westering sun, until clouds of silver steam from a factory blot them out, and the sun lights up the landscape with a rather harsh light, staining fields and woods with a paintbox intensity.

Soon the royal party reached the region of the Spessart, very hilly and wooded, where the post chaise was forced to slow down; eventually they had

All her life Queen Victoria was fascinated by regional costumes, and these examples from around Coburg were as carefully preserved in her albums as any paintings of palaces. (Watercolour by Rothbart.)

to get out and walk up the longest hill. This conjures up a curious image: the Queen of England trudging along in the dust on this pilgrimage to her husband's birthplace. The bond between them was powerful indeed, to draw her over six hundred miles, far away from duty to her country and from her home and children.

Today the motorway cuts through the forests of the Spessart, striding for mile after mile over wooded hills and deep valleys as though in seven-league boots. The modern traveller is able to cover unthinkable numbers of miles in a day and to cross in the blinking of an eye steep gorges and wide rivers. At Lengfurt Victoria and Albert stepped into a ferry to cross the Main, the carriage crossing in one ferry and the royal party in another; their own, noted the Queen, was 'very smartly arranged'.[31]

The autobahn comes sweeping down to skirt Würzburg, where the Queen spent the next night. From the motorway you see dramatic new tower blocks and away to the left the long walls of Marienberg, looking like a toy fortress on the western escarpment above the river. There is no sign at all that in the centre of the town is the Residenz, possibly one of the grandest palaces in the whole of Germany, built between 1720 and 1744 by the prince-bishops of Würzburg on a scale that would dwarf Versailles.

Here once more is the hand of Balthasar Neumann, who designed a staircase so enormous that it makes Brühl look small by comparison. Neumann's critics said that the vast ceiling which spans it would never stand up, so he challenged them to drive a cannon to the bottom of the staircase and fire it. No one took him up on his offer, and Tiepolo painted this daring vault with a fresco of Apollo enthroned in splendour among the continents of the world.

At the top of the staircase Queen Victoria found 'a very magnificent saloon of immense height and size, the ceiling entirely painted in fresco. On each side of this room there is an endless suite of very fine rooms; I am sure we had 12 or 14!!'[32] Splendidly lodged she might have been, but Queen Victoria did not pass a very comfortable night. She arrived after her eleven-hour journey with a racking headache; some of their servants and most of their luggage had not yet arrived, so 'we had to get to bed as we could'.[33]

Today the visitor can pace the inlaid floors, stiff-necked and mouth agape at the fantasies depicted on walls and ceilings, astounded by the scale, dazzled by the glamour, vision blurring as dimensional and logical boundaries are crossed and re-crossed: a painted cloak overhangs the cornice and becomes three-dimensional, supported by cherubs – or are they hanging on to it for dear life? Is

The magnificent Residenz at Würzburg in the 1840s, where Queen Victoria spent the second night of her journey from the Rhine to Coburg. Although today it all appears to be just as it was when she described it, the Residenz suffered severely in the Second World War and has been almost completely rebuilt. (Watercolour; artist unknown.)

the painting turning into sculpture or is the sculpture emerging from the painting? Gilded Corinthian capitals swirl with vegetation like herbaceous borders in a gale, fat cherubs struggle to hold up ceilings, cartouches of quails and dancing girls are painted on gilded shutters; there are so many sumptuous and varied rooms of looking-glass and gold, of chinoiserie and lacquer, that the cumulative effect is quite overwhelming.

Just when you feel completely sated with baroque excess, the route takes you along the corridors behind these state rooms, past a harrowing series of photographs which show blackened walls, gaping roofs, empty window casements, shattered plasterwork and broken doorways choked with rubble. Würzburg was bombed on 16 March 1945, only a few months before the end of the war, and incendiaries left much of the Residenz little more than a shell.

Neumann's artillery-proof ceiling survived the attack, but realization dawns slowly on the visitor that virtually everything else on view has been restored: the Residenz has risen like a phoenix from its ashes. This painstaking work of renewal seems somehow more poignant than the blackened rubble of destruction. If the glories of the Residenz had simply been swept away it would have been a fearful loss, but not perhaps as moving as the expression of resilience and strength and spirit in the restitution of beauty destroyed.

Through traffic is most effectively channelled out of towns and villages between Würzburg and Coburg, and the roads that Queen Victoria used are in many places deserted little country lanes. But her journal records everything, all the places where they changed horses (some the merest hamlets), the landmarks they passed, even what the weather was like. With a copy of this extraordinarily accurate document it is possible, in this unchanged corner of Germany, to follow her route very closely, so that her voice becomes your guide.

The Queen crossed the Main (for the third time) at Kitzingen. This is a particularly difficult place to negotiate and we can sympathize with her comment, 'we went very slow this stage'.[34] The countryside here is open, with wide, rolling, ploughed fields patched with stands of woodland. You can see for miles. Every so often red roofs and white triangular gables of cosy villages huddle round tall, creamy church spires capped with onion domes.

We start to climb through beautiful woods (yes, here it is in the journal: 'The country fine and woody', says the Queen).[35] We drive along a shallow, winding valley and come to a green copper dome with a flaming gold spire on top, a little village clustered at the edge of the woods, a rather grand monastery and a honey-coloured arch across the road: 'We passed by Kloster Ebrach', wrote Queen Victoria, 'where there is a very fine church and a deserted convent'.[36]

Where the Queen did not look carefully at her surroundings, Albert made sure she saw what she should: 'Dearest Albert made me observe several Storks' nests on the chimneys of houses, & one stork sitting on one.'[37] She admired the 'curious' and 'picturesque' old town of Bamberg, its women in bright red kerchiefs, and her escort of Bavarian Light Horse, very smart in dark green and pink. We find ouselves spinning past on the bypass, and have to crane our necks for a glimpse of Bamberg's twin spires.

Heading north from the town, Albert pointed out to the Queen, as she later noted, 'the Einsiedeln, a very fine mountain to the right, at the foot of which is the famous church of Vierzehn Heiligen, which is very fine and renowned for a famous pilgrimage, which takes place there on Ascension day'.[38] This had been a holy place since a visionary herdsman at the time of Joan of Arc had seen the Infant Jesus in the midst of the Fourteen Saints of Intercession. The present church is the work of none other than Balthasar Neumann, his interior here so ornate and sumptuous that he called it 'God's ballroom'. On reading in the Queen's journal that Banz Abbey stands on the opposite hill, we look up to the left and, sure enough, there is its splendid silhouette.

Mönchroden, outside Coburg. (Watercolour attributed to Max Bruckner.) The bright colours of painted landscapes such as this seemed unlikely until we found ourselves surrounded by them in reality.

So far on her journey the weather had not smiled on Queen Victoria, and most of this second day in the chaise had been wet, which 'put us quite into despair, for dear Coburg',[39] but then it cleared up and the Queen 'began to feel so moved, so agitated in coming near the Coburg frontier'.[40]

She had come a long way and was approaching the goal of her journey, and it is impossible not to feel a corresponding excitement as we hurry on, our car eating up the miles. We leave behind a village daydreaming round a duck pond where the houses nestle up to the stone walls of a castle whose armorial bearings are carved over the doorway. We speed on, past strips of reddish plough, where birds of prey hover over the newly turned earth and there are no hedges. Beyond, the plump wooded hills are touched with autumn. It all looks exactly like the pictures we saw when we opened the souvenir albums in the Royal Library.

Along the horizon marches a dense, frowning line of trees, the outskirts of the Thüringer Wald, the forests of Thuringia, as old as folk tales, where you would not be surprised to see wild boar or a dappled stag. These forests are haunted now by the ghosts of the generations severed by the Iron Curtain which ran a bare twenty kilometres away. We have come to what was, until very recently, the end of Western Europe.

We find, with some difficulty, the place where we are to stay, Schloss Neuhof (now a hotel), which once belonged to the Coburg family and was visited by Queen Victoria on several occasions. The weather is closing in. The schloss is not far from the town, tucked away in a valley, its tall, yellow turrets protruding over the treetops, and as the rainy mist sprinkles over us we have the feeling that little has changed here with the passage of time.

CHAPTER THREE

The
Land of
Albert's Birth, 1845

The Ehrenburg Palace and the Veste

When Victoria and Albert arrived in Coburg in August 1845 they were given a series of welcomes. Albert's brother, Ernst II, the reigning duke (always known to the Queen as Ernest), himself met them a little way out of the town, which he entered with them. The carriage procession passed between cheering crowds, decorations, garlands and archways, through narrow streets where the houses overhang as if looking down to see who is passing underneath, and came at last to a large palace, the Ehrenburg, right in the centre of Coburg. Here Victoria and Albert found the rest of the family 'en grande tenue', gathered to welcome them: 'the staircase was *full* of *cousins*',[1] exclaimed the Queen, thoroughly enjoying this 'very affecting but beautiful moment'.[2]

Today, in the dusk, the only figures on the vast echoing staircase are cold, swathed statues, casts from the antique, but in a small antechamber upstairs, known as the Family Hall, we come face to face with the most important members of the Coburg family.

Two of the paintings need no introduction and we meet them with a happy little shock of recognition: these are copies of the portraits by Franz Xaver Winterhalter of Victoria and Albert, done in 1846 or 1847, the Queen plump and rosy, with the Prince of Wales at her side, Prince Albert looking handsome, sober and statesmanlike. Victoria and Albert both belong here by rights of pedigree, for the Queen was as much a Coburg as her husband, who was also her first cousin.

In a rather dark corner is the gentle face of their grandfather, Duke Franz Anton of Saxe-Coburg Saalfeld, the passionate collector who was more interested in his prints and drawings than his duchy, which at the end of the eighteenth century was one of the poorest in Germany. By then it had been impoverished by a long history of wars (usually other people's), mismanage-

The entry of Queen
Victoria and Prince
Albert, accompanied by
the King and the Queen
of the Belgians, into the
town of Coburg,
19 August 1845.
(Watercolour by
Rothbart.)

ment, neglect and disputes over inheritance. The duke left most of the business
of ruling to his long-nosed, capable wife, born Princess Auguste Reuss zu
Ebersdorf, whose portrait is here too. She bore him nine children, of whom
three sons and four daughters survived. It was the careers of these children that
made the family famous. By the end of the nineteenth century they had
descendants on the thrones of Germany, England, Belgium, Spain, Bulgaria,
Rumania, Russia and Sweden and had even, briefly, made a disastrous imperial
excursion into Mexico.

The family fortunes began to go up in the world when in 1796 there came a
summons from that elderly despot Catherine the Great, who was anxious to
find a wife for her nephew, the Grand Duke Constantine. Already an alcoholic
at sixteen, he seemed to be going to the bad, and she hoped that a German

The Ehrenburg, formal residence of the dukes of Coburg, in the centre of the town, as it was in 1846. (Watercolour by W. Corden.)

princess (Catherine herself being German) might have a good influence on him. The Duchess of Saxe-Coburg Saalfeld packed her three eldest daughters into a coach and set off with them on the six weeks' journey to St Petersburg. Catherine chose the youngest, Juliane.

It was a very unhappy marriage, but was responsible for the rise of the House of Coburg because Juliane invited her handsome brothers, Ernst and Leopold, to St Petersburg. They became colonels of the guard, and after the battle of Waterloo Leopold accompanied the Tsar, Alexander I, to London. There he met the daughter of the Prince Regent, Princess Charlotte, heir to the

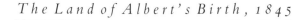

English throne, whom he married in 1816. When she died in childbirth a year later Leopold's happiness was cut short, but the Coburgs did provide England with an heir and Leopold's influence in England endured: it was his sister Victoria who married Edward, Duke of Kent and in 1819 made the heroic journey to England to give birth to Princess Victoria, to whom Uncle Leopold was like a second father. The Duchess of Kent, King Leopold and his second wife, Louise of Orléans, were all in Coburg for Queen Victoria's visit.

The painting which dominates the Family Hall is a vast canvas of Duke Ernst I, Prince Albert's father, looking like Byron's understudy, draped in ermine and scarlet velvet, with the unfinished façade of the Ehrenburg behind him. He inherited the duchy in 1806 during the harsh period of the Napoleonic

'When I came across this painting, which is a copy of Winterhalter's portrait, of the Queen holding the little Prince of Wales's hand, in the Family Hall of the Ehrenburg, it made me think how fortunate I am in having a close relationship with my daughters, and how much I value the cosy world that we share at story-time each evening.'

Wars, but he did very well out of the Congress of Vienna, and as soon as times were more settled, and the French had begun to pay reparations, he set about beautifying Coburg. He rebuilt and restored most of the ducal buildings, including, of course, the Ehrenburg.

This had originally been a Franciscan monastery and had been enlarged and turned into a ducal palace in the 1540s, but it had seen no major works since the 1690s. Duke Ernst had grand ideas and wanted his principal residence to have a dignity that enhanced his own. Between 1810 and 1840 the palace was given a gothic facelift and completely remodelled after drawings by Karl Friedrich Schinkel. The extensive modernizations inside, which were in the French Empire style, were overseen by André-Marie Renié-Grétry in close association with the duke.

Queen Victoria's journal describing her arrival in Coburg, 19 August 1845, copied by Princess Beatrice, with the Queen's sketch of peasant women in traditional costumes.

Under Duke Ernst Coburg was equipped with everything a duke might need and all of it is still there: it has a town palace, summer residences, a court garden planted in the naturalistic, English style, and a court theatre conveniently close to the palace. Albert's father left a definitive stamp on the face of the town, but Coburgers, who are otherwise most generous with details of their ducal history, become evasive on the subject of Duke Ernst: 'there are certain stories about him' is all they will say, for this connoisseur prince, who had done so much for Coburg, was also a libertine and debauchee. His habits did not change after he married Albert's mother, Princess Louise of Saxe-Altenburg, when he was thirty-three and she a child of sixteen. After the birth of Prince Albert, her second son, she made the mistake of taking comfort outside the bounds of a loveless marriage. Duke Ernst divorced her. Later, adding incest to injury, he married his niece, Marie von Württemberg.

In spite of it all, Prince Albert loved his dissolute father and wept when Duke Ernst left England after his wedding. The duke died in 1844 and a year later, on her arrival in Coburg, Queen Victoria gave extravagant expression to the feelings she shared with her husband: 'our beloved Papa, oh! *how* does every sound, every view, every step I take, make us think of him and feel an indescribable, hopeless longing for him!'[3]

Across the room from Duke Ernst is the portrait of his niece-wife. She looks rather more glamorous here than she evidently did on the day when she formed part of Victoria's welcoming committee on the Ehrenburg stairs. When the Queen saw her for the first time she wrote, 'Mama Marie looks much older than I expected, and is enormously fat, but has fine features and was so extremely kind to me.'[4]

On the wall opposite Queen Victoria and Prince Albert hangs the portrait of yet another Coburg success: the King Consort of Portugal. Ferdinand was their first cousin and had once been a possible contender for Queen Victoria's hand, but instead he married Maria da Gloria, Queen of Portugal, who is next to him; not even the most desperate court painter's flattery can disguise her bulk. They represent the Catholic line of the Coburgs.

This family gathering would not be complete without Albert's brother Ernest. He inherited a great many of his father's characteristics, and his excesses left him unable to father a child. His long-suffering wife, Princess Alexandrine of Baden, whom he married in 1842, gazes shyly out from her portrait in a cloud of lace, looking, just as Queen Victoria said she did, 'like a rose, and so retiring'.[5] A much later description of her, by a disrespectful but fond great-niece, concluded with her 'depressed-looking nose, hopelessly pear shaped'. By then she had become 'A sad old figure whose one and only love was the terrible old gentleman who treated her as no one else would dare treat a servant.'[6]

The Ehrenburg was used by the dukes for formal entertaining, and on the same floor is the hall where some of the gayest scenes of Queen Victoria's first visit took place. This is the Hall of the Giants, where twenty-eight muscular plasterwork Atlases stand round the walls as though waiting to take part in a Mr Universe competition. Each holds a golden candelabra with one hand and with the other either supports the heavily ornate ceiling or embraces his muscular neighbour: 'a handsome large room', said the Queen, 'supported by giants terminating in a pedestal'.[7]

The Queen of England had met all her extended family; now the society of Coburg must be presented. The Queen put on a red crêpe de Chine gown, a wreath of natural flowers and her diamonds, and stood beneath the giants in a row with the rest of the family while Ernest and Alexandrine made the introductions. The Queen was impressed: the Coburgers 'behaved so well, making much better bows than *any* of our people at the Levées'.[8] She thought it had all been very well managed. Duty done, royalty was free to amuse itself,

'*Nothing could be better done than it is here; the Court is so dignified – the whole* cuisine *so good – the equipages and horses so fine – the theatre – everything, is* so well *done; we* could not *do it* better.'

22 AUGUST 1845

Ehrenburg's Hall of the Giants, which dates from the 1690s and was used by the dukes for court festivities, banquets, balls and theatrical performances. It is still used for concerts today. The watercolour, by Rothbart, shows the room as it was when Queen Victoria danced here with her cousins. The ceiling decoration of painted clouds and ascending eagles has since been removed to reveal the original painting.

The market place, Coburg, in the 1840s. Now, as in Albert's boyhood, the smoke from the bratwurst sellers' fires still billows in fragrant clouds through the heart of the town. (Watercolour; artist unknown.)

and the next evening the Queen dressed in a light blue tarlatan gown trimmed with lace, and in the company of some two or three hundred people, including all her royal cousins, she danced the night away. Lady Canning heard 'great approbation expressed at the Queen's hearty dancing, & I suppose she enjoyed it exceedingly as she allows herself to gallop, valse, & polk [sic] with her cousins, she went on incessantly till the ball ended'.[9] Queen Victoria did enjoy it exceedingly, and when she sat down to supper felt quite sure that 'nothing could be better done than it is here; the Court is so dignified – the whole dinner and *cuisine* so good'. In short, 'everything is *so well* done; *we* could *not* do it *better*'.[10]

In the empty hall music still seems to hang in the air and the giants lean out in frozen animation. We cross the wide acreage of lattice-work parquet and lean on a windowsill; it is practically at chin height, and you have to clamber up to reach the window catch. It is like being a child again or finding yourself in the house of a giant.

Outside, the uneven red roofs of the town float, undulating gently beneath a soft pink sky, and shadows are gathering in the cobbled street below. It is easy

'As soon as I saw this view (below, right) I knew it would be perfect to paint. I did not realize then that Queen Victoria had once thought so too. Next to her sketch (below, left) she wrote "From my sitting room window, market day Oct 3 1860", it is also signed by her daughter Victoria.'

to feel that we have dipped back in time, to any one of Queen Victoria's seven visits, from the first, in 1845, to the last, forty-nine years later, in 1894. The sun rests on the red and white oriel window of the Stadthaus and the onion dome on the tower of one of the town gates beyond it. We are looking straight down into a scene painted by the Queen at the Ehrenburg, which is preserved in one of the shabby green sketchbooks in the Royal Library. She had marked it, 'From my sitting room window, market day Oct 3 1860'. Before we leave the hall we take a quick look at a plaque commemorating the widowed Queen's meeting here in 1863 with Franz Joseph, Emperor of Austria, an encounter which she described as 'very very trying for me in every way'.[11]

The Ehrenburg is a vast maze. The shining floors go on for ever, inlaid with seven kinds of wood (woodworking was a speciality of the region). We look into the Gobelins room, where a courageous seventeenth-century duchess had slept under the menacing weight of one of the heaviest ceilings in Germany. Ernst I ripped out a lot of the room's baroque decoration to make hanging space for his fine French tapestries of the New Indies series. Behind a bloody representation of lions attacking deer is

'The Ehrenburg was used by the dukes of Coburg for formal occasions and you can still see today the very rooms that Queen Victoria visited. I was fascinated by how easy it was to dip back into their period; there was a definite atmosphere of Queen Victoria and Albert here and it was a very good feeling to be in Albert's childhood home.'

a bulge in the wall where a lift was installed for Queen Victoria long after her dancing days were done, when she had become too old and stiff to manage stairs.

At last we find ourselves in the long series of rooms which perfectly preserve the trappings of an early nineteenth-century German court, modelled by Ernst I on the pomp of Napoleon's empire. Built before unification, when Germany was still a number of small sovereign kingdoms, this little court survived the nineteenth century and the changes that later dukes might have wanted to make, it survived the ruin of two world wars, and here it all is, frozen in time. A chill wind blows down the icy enfilade. The arms of the House of Wettin are inlaid in the floor of an antechamber just to remind weary supplicants who they were waiting for. We pass into the throne room, heavy with red velvet and gilded bay leaves. The canopy over the great red sofa is crowned with heron feathers dyed in the colours of the House of Coburg. The French Empire style is stiff and grand, cold and formal; we pass on through an audience chamber of snuff brown and blue, just as it appears in the painting in the souvenir album, and reach the duke's sitting room, where the furniture is

Audience room in the
Ehrenburg, deep frozen
in time. The decoration
and furniture, mainly
French, dates from the
early 1820s when Albert's
father modernized many
of the interiors.
(Watercolour, above,
by F. Rothbart.)

The duke's sitting room in the Ehrenburg, with the swan-headed furniture which was probably copied in Coburg from models bought in France in 1815.

ornamented with gilded swans' heads. Sitting in the window here before she dressed for the ball in the Hall of the Giants, Queen Victoria wrote: 'The evening was so clear and bright and beautiful the view from the writing table, which stands in the window, is most beautiful, of the Festung, which is close above the town and the Place in front, with the Theatre, is so pretty.'[12]

The public rooms may not have changed, but the bedroom next door looks very different from the way it did in 1845. The archways have gone, the elegant, striped wallpaper was replaced in about 1860 with a design of fat brown flowers, and the most striking feature of the room is now a large mahogany water closet, one of the first, and probably the most famous, to be installed in any German palace. It is of English make, and was put in at about the time of the Queen's visit in 1860. Everywhere the cold strikes to the bone; it is a long time since silent servants went up and down the passages behind these rooms, filling up the stoves that kept German rooms so very much hotter than Queen Victoria thought comfortable or healthy.

A thin tinkling of music comes from the piano in the duke's sitting room, a

The same room as it would have looked when it was used by Queen Victoria. (Watercolour; artist unknown.)

ghostly echo of the times so long ago when all was warmth and light, and the chandeliers, which hang now like frozen waterfalls, sparkled with lights.

Victoria and Albert did not stay in the Ehrenburg in 1845, but they used these rooms as a base between entertainments: 'established ourselves in the 3 pretty rooms which belonged to poor dear Papa & where Ernest and Alexandrine now live. A bedroom, charming little library & sort of bathroom, where dear Albert dressed.'[13]

The charming little library is the very essence of Duke Ernst I. It is built of

satinwood in the form of a Greek temple, and is said to have housed his collection of French novels. Here a certain wariness will come over the Coburger's expression; they were very fine books, you understand, beautifully printed and bound, with particularly fine engravings, but books 'of a certain peculiar bent'.

But the entertainments which Albert and Ernest arranged for the Queen's pleasure were innocent indeed and she thoroughly enjoyed them. The children's festival with a procession, dances, and dinner for the Feast of

St Gregory was 'the prettiest thing I ever saw'.[14] Three evenings she went to the theatre across the way, 'an extremely pretty one, painted with blue, white, and gold'[15] (her description still holds good), and watched with pleasure an opera, a tragedy and a 'historical comedy'. Her ladies, whose German was less fluent, found it very hard to stay awake. On the Sunday that she was in Coburg she attended service in the Moritz Kirche, just behind the Ehrenburg, which has a bit of everything about it: a gothic chancel, a baroque altarpiece, an outrageous gilded pulpit, a classical nave and a pretty plasterwork ceiling better suited to a drawing room. Here the Queen was welcomed as 'the great Christian Queen, descended from the Saxon Dukes, who were the first Reformers' in the church where 'the Reformation was first preached'.[16]

We emerge from the Ehrenburg cold and hungry (the Coburg welcome is warm and friendly but the palace is like an iceberg) and walk round the corner into the market square. The old buildings are painted in bright colours, a few people are standing about waiting for buses, and in the middle of the cobbled square stands the statue of Albert which Queen Victoria erected to his memory in 1865. She would have recognized the scene immediately, and probably the smell, too, coming in clouds of blue smoke from two stalls parked close under Albert, where the bratwurst sellers are grilling sausages over glowing embers of fir cones. Queen Victoria sent out from the Ehrenburg for these famous sausages from the market, and drank 'some of the excellent Coburg beer to it – they are so good'.[17] Standing in the square we try them too. Lost in the tranquil, changeless scene, we gaze at the little houses with attic windows set into red roofs, and the pigeons cooing and squabbling round the statue; a few incurious passers-by continue on their way without a second glance at us.

It is growing misty. Each street light has a luminous halo, and buildings are no more than presences. We drive through the narrow streets and begin to climb. What a pull it must have been for carriages. The higher we go, the thicker grows the mist. Trees planted by Duke Ernst in the Hofgarten loom up and disappear behind us; the road is covered in fallen leaves. All of a sudden, above us tower a shadowy bastion, a ghostly rampart and a bridge which appears to arch out into nowhere over an invisible abyss. We hesitate, 'Can we?' 'Yes, go on'. The car noses forward over the bridge, and just as we think we are going to drive out into thin air we are swallowed up by a narrow tunnel. We emerge into a pleasant courtyard where half-timbered buildings with steep red roofs look welcoming and homely across green lawns and cobbled pathways. A man like a vole pops his head out of a window surrounded by geraniums, waving a shaving mirror, and directs us into an inner courtyard.

The children's fête on the Anger, an entertainment which Albert knew that his wife would enjoy. (Watercolour by H. J. Schneider.)

The fortress, or Veste, as it is today, its silhouette slightly rearranged by restoration and war damage, but still dominating the countryside for miles around.

We are right inside the fortress of Coburg, the Festung that Queen Victoria had seen through the window from her writing table. Known today as the Veste, it stands five hundred feet above the town in one of the largest fortified strongholds in the whole of Germany. Its origins are lost in pre-history, but more recently – say, for the last thousand years – it has had just the kind of history you would expect of such a place. It has housed the rulers of Coburg, who could see from its ramparts what was going on across most of Franconia and Thuringia. It has sheltered Martin Luther, the man at the eye of a storm of religious controversy which split the whole of Europe. It has withstood sieges with gallantry, and then fallen through treachery. For a while it served as a prison and it has known centuries of ruin and neglect.

When Prince Albert brought Queen Victoria up here in 1845 it had recently been rescued from dereliction by Duke Ernst I, ardent devotee of the romantic revival, who not only had restored it but had been unable to resist the temptation to recreate it as he thought it should have been. The Queen was all admiration for the results. The armoury was crammed with beautiful armour, artistically arranged. In Luther's room there were still parts of the reformer's

The same view, showing the fortress as it was in the mid-nineteenth century, by T. Rothbart. On 20 August 1845 the Queen looked out on 'a glorious and *most* extensive view . . . Coburg below, with the Thüringer Wald and all the fine mountains towards Gotha in the background is quite beautiful; and there is such a constant movement in the ground, it looked quite Italian.'

bedstead and chair, 'most precious relics',[18] and where the duke had added and embellished the Queen noted that 'The old and new carving is so beautifully matched, that it is all in keeping.'[19] She was much intrigued by the Horn Room, where the hunting exploits of the sixteenth-century Johann Casimir, first Duke of Saxe-Coburg, were depicted in sixty wooden inlaid pictures round the panelled walls. It all had a fashionably historic-exotic flavour, even down to the inmates of the bastions: 'We looked down', wrote the Queen, 'at the two bears who are always kept here, and fed them with paper!!'[20]

It was all as much a stage set for scenes from Queen Victoria's own ancestry as for Albert's, and here in Coburg this most famous of England's royal couples could feel that they were stepping back into their common heritage.

Later restorers of the Veste have interpreted the past differently, and they, as well as stray bombs in 1945, have done much to alter the appearance of the place as Queen Victoria knew it. In many ways it was much more colourful then – and that is not just the impression which the Queen's enthusiastic account gives us. The souvenir albums show richly gilded and ornate 'medievalized' interiors, in particular the chamber of Martin Luther, where he

The armoury in the Veste, *c.*1860; medieval arms and weaponry arranged in the nineteenth century to summon up an idealized past. (Watercolour by Rothbart.)

stayed during the Diet of Augsburg and continued his controversial work of translating the Bible into German. We brave a labyrinth of passageways and massive stone stairs to find that Luther's room is now a low, bare cell of plain wood and whitewash. Perhaps we like our history more unadorned than the nineteenth century did.

Similarly, the old watercolour of the armoury shows it much as Queen Victoria must have seen it, but, although the enormous collection of weaponry and armour is all still there, it is no longer in a glorious, romantic muddle, having been identified, catalogued, and in effect sanitized. The suits of armour stand in ranks behind glass barriers, the two knights on horseback no longer caracole gaily across the back of the hall but have been put into glass cases, and you can see that the horses are stuffed. There is still a Bear Bastion, but no bears. The Horn Room is being treated for woodworm.

Down in the cellars, however, under ponderous stone vaulting, we do find the 'very fine and curious old Bridal Carriages of John Casimir'.[21] These are two long, low, ornately gilded carriages; the combination of golden lions holding up ducal coats of arms, the treasure-chest shape of the carved body, and the red cartwheels make them look at once primitive and splendid. They are apparently in full working order, and look as if they could rumble out to

Martin Luther's room in the Veste, *c.*1860, lavishly decorated by Prince Albert's father in the style then considered appropriate to honour the memory of the most famous occupant of the fortress. (Watercolour by Rothbart.) Luther's room today is plain and bare.

another wedding tomorrow. There is something very odd about standing in front of an object so rich and strange and imagining the small, vivacious personage of Queen Victoria looking at it in curiosity as well.

It is impossible to admire the bridal coaches without having your attention drawn to the quite extraordinary figures assembled across the way: Ceres, Neptune, a beautiful bare-breasted Indian, a black unicorn, a phoenix, a griffin, a calf. What *are* these creatures, beautiful and sinister, like the avenging figures that might pursue you through a nightmare?

It takes a little while to work out that they are carved figureheads attached to sleighs, and that each has a matching horse collar and a harness hung up on the wall behind it. These are the vehicles for a game known as the Damen Carousel, which was enjoyed by the ladies of the sixteenth- and seventeenth-century court in Coburg (perhaps the duchess who braved the heavy ceiling would have played it). They did not need snow to play – pine needles would be scattered over a wooden floor – and those sharp lances that are now propped up beside each sleigh were aimed at a target.

We leave the Veste behind us. Looking back, it seems as if the tall ramparts, which have known so many secrets, draw the mists about themselves once again as the fortress broods on its hilltop, watching over the town below.

The 'dear Rosenau'

It is a very cold, crisp morning and the sky is an absolutely clear crystal blue. A light hoar frost dusts the fields, and the woods are shining bronze and gold. We can see our breath. The early sun sends long fingers up the meadow ahead of us to the little creamy-white building at the top of the slope. The bare branches of neighbouring trees cast a tracery of shadows across its pale, stepped gable and green shutters, and the sunshine glints off the little panes in the pointed windows. A single evergreen tree stands beside the round tower which protrudes from the side of the building, giving it a jaunty air as though it is wearing a feather in its cap.

So this is the Rosenau, the house where Albert was born and spent the happiest times of his childhood. It was here that he brought his wife to stay in 1845, so that his birthplace became her resting place, the goal of her journey, and of ours also. Without a visit to the Rosenau our quest would be incomplete. For a moment or two time seems suspended and the past feels very close. We are lost for words, just dreaming of a young husband proudly showing his wife all the places that were dear to his childhood, everything they saw together transformed by love. The leaves fall around us like rain, making coppery pools of colour on the grass.

The Rosenau is a modest cradle for a great prince. There are no lordly gates on the high road to announce its presence to the world, only an avenue of fine chestnuts. It discloses its gentle charms gradually.

It is only about four miles out of Coburg, hidden away among the trees in the surrounding park, which is laid out in the informal, English style. The house is not large, and has only a single staircase, which curls up inside the round tower and leads to the living rooms which are all on the first floor. It is a castle of human proportions. The ceilings are relatively low, perhaps twelve

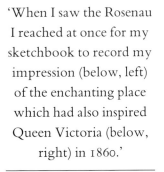

'When I saw the Rosenau I reached at once for my sketchbook to record my impression (below, left) of the enchanting place which had also inspired Queen Victoria (below, right) in 1860.'

'It was a magical morning when I arrived at the Rosenau, where
Albert was born, and where he and Queen Victoria stayed in 1845. I
drifted off into a dream, feeling very close to them, and imagining
Albert's pride and delight in showing it all to his young wife, just
like my own gallant husband, who swept me with such panache
through the corridors of his childhood haunts.
It seemed to me here at Rosenau so comfortable to understand the
passion Queen Victoria had for Albert and her hunger
to know all the intricate details, with the burning feeling of love
that holds no barrier.'

The sitting room in the Rosenau which Queen Victoria used. The Rosenau has recently been restored, with the help of these watercolours (above, by F. Rothbart), and the home of Albert's childhood is once more bright and friendly.

The bedroom at the Rosenau where Queen Victoria awoke on her first morning here, '*how* happy and *how joyful*'. Where the original furniture that was once in these rooms no longer exists, similar pieces have been installed. (Watercolour by F. Rothbart.)

'I felt as if I should like always to live here with my dearest Albert, and if I was not what I am — this would have been my real home.'

20 AUGUST 1845

feet high, and the walls are painted with neo-gothic patterns rather than ornamented with elaborate plasterwork and carving. The floors are of simple wood parquet. It is easy to understand why Victoria should have loved this place so much; its simplicity was an escape from her duties as Queen, but the clearest ghost in the Rosenau is the still powerful trace of the unqualified love that she lavished on Albert. It is a happy place.

As always, Queen Victoria described it all in such detail that you can follow her round the house. We turn left at the top of the stairs and find ourselves in her little dressing room, pink and grey, with a scattering of painted oak leaves round the alcove for the porcelain stove. Next door is 'our dear little bedroom', whose walls the colour of a summer's night are decorated with entwined convolvulus and fluttering butterflies; it is just big enough for one crowned bed hung with gauzy curtains. Beyond is 'my sitting room a very nice room with four windows'.[22] Painted arches, a network of interlocking patterns on the ceiling and very smart, plain, glossy black furniture make this room friendly, feminine and intimate, and remind us that the Rosenau was one of the summer retreats from the formalities of life in the Ehrenburg. The windows look out over a little terrace garden — with a fountain, rose beds, urns and battlements — to the green fields beyond, and the valley which runs north towards the blue line of wooded hills and the old Iron Curtain.

At the Rosenau the Queen was at her most private, and her happiest. In these little rooms she made herself comfortable on the evening she arrived, and dressed for dinner before crossing the central passage and going into the drawing room, '*en suite*, just opposite my little room'.[23] Here, beneath a cobweb of painted hexagons converging on the centre of a bright green ceiling, a large gathering of Victoria's and Albert's German cousins assembled on that first night in the Rosenau, on Tuesday, 19 August 1845.

Preceded by two court officials bearing staffs of office, the assembled family ('like the whole Almanach de Gotha alive',[24] said Lady Canning) wound down the staircase — as you descend, you sense the crush of wide skirts, the bowing and the curtseying and

Banquet at the Rosenau: 'everything very handsome;' observed the Queen on 19 August 1845, 'exceedingly well done and well served and *bien grand*. Much better served than at the King of Prussia's.'

The Marmorsaal, or marble hall, at the Rosenau, where Albert was christened. (Watercolour, above, by F. Rothbart.) The Queen had only been here a short while before she felt completely at home, almost as though she had spent her own childhood here. At the Rosenau we too had a sense, as nowhere else, that we had reached our journey's goal.

the punctilious precedence – to the Rosenau's principal room, known as the Marmorsaal (though its so-called marble is in fact polished plaster), at the bottom of the house. It was a room of special delight for the Queen, for here Albert had been christened. Cool and graceful, its vaults and columns might almost have been carved out of ice and seamed with fiery veins of gold, and it was lit with delicate fretwork candelabra like little firework explosions.

Here they dined, the Queen observing briskly: 'the table was in the shape of a horseshoe, and everything very handsome; exceedingly well done and well served and *bien grand*. Much better served than at the King of Prussia's.'[25] Like most travellers, she was interested in new and different customs: 'The serving in Germany is totally different to ours. There are *no* dishes placed on the table except the dessert (which is there the whole time) and there are no separate courses whatever. Each dish is brought to you separately one after the other, the meat cut, but left on the dish for you to take a piece from.'[26]

The Queen sat between Ernest and the Grand Duke of Baden (Alexandrine's father) who, though 'very kind and civil', was inexplicably 'rather embarrassed'.[27] Queen Victoria was never too tired to take in, and candidly record, the distinguishing quirks of the people she was meeting,

The sitting room at the Rosenau which Albert used. (Watercolour by F. Rothbart.)

particularly when they were members of her own or Albert's family whom she had never seen before. Besides, there were so many changes to observe in the cousins she had already met, and her journal is peppered with notes on which one had grown grey or fat, acquired moustaches or become more like his mother. But the travellers were tired, and that first evening was necessarily brief; they retired early to rest.

The next morning Queen Victoria's cup of joy overflowed:

How happy, and *how joyful* we felt on awaking to feel ourselves *here*, at the *dear* Rosenau, my dearest Albert's birthplace – and favourite place! – I told him I was *so delighted* so *over happy*, so *overthankful* – to be able to come here at last which we *so* wished – and which we *so* feared would never be the case. I felt as if I should like always to live here with my dearest Albert, and if I was not what I am – *this* would have been my real home. But I shall always consider it *my* second home and as *my second country*. My dearest Albert was *so so* happy to be here with me – it is like a beautiful dream.[28]

There was so much to see. Albert showed her all over the house. On the same floor as her apartments were 'my dearest Albert's 2 rooms – his dressing

'At first it seemed a violation to read through Queen Victoria's personal thoughts, but the strong spirit of love still lingering in these enchanted rooms drew me in, and it became clear to me that I had fallen under the spell of Queeen Victoria's unqualified love for her "dearest Albert". She was happiest, and most private, here.'

room which was poor dear Papa's bedroom with his bed and everything left in it just as it was – and a sitting room which is just as poor dear Papa used to have it; on his writing table are the pens with ink in them, just as he left them! And so they must remain, they are quite sacred to us.'[29] It is a curious sensation to be reading Queen Victoria's words in the very room that she was describing. With the morning sun pouring in through the windows on to the pages of her journal, a sense of peace expands and fills the room.

Although the pens and other relics of 'poor dear Papa' have been swept away long since, you can still see much of the furniture which Duke Ernst I chose for the Rosenau when he turned this medieval building, which goes back to at least 1439, into a ducal residence shortly after the Napoleonic Wars had ended. The influence of Schinkel can be felt in the modernization. Almost all the furniture comes from Vienna, where the duke had attended the Congress, and it was designed by Ferdinand Hasselbrinck and Josef Dannhauser.

In 1817 Duke Ernst had married Princess Louise of Saxe-Altenburg, and the event was celebrated with a mock tournament in the meadow below the Rosenau. The recently renovated building quickly became the duchess's favourite residence, and it was here that she gave birth to her second son,

Albert, not in the room with the trellis of convolvulus but in one upstairs, which was used in 1845 by Albert's secretary, Anson. Of course the Queen ran up – on Albert's birthday – to have a look at it. She had to go higher still, to the top of the house, to see the room in which Albert had lived 'right up to the last moment', before he came to England to marry her. Up in the roof, where vast timbers lean over you, each one hewn from a forest giant, and where each floorboard is as wide as a table, it is like being inside a great wooden ship. You are left in no doubt that the Rosenau is solidly built of the finest materials – but then, that is no more than you would expect of a building which had once belonged to the Masters of the Coburg Mint.

The Queen wrote of Ernest and Albert's old room that it 'is quite in the roof, with a small little bedroom on each side, in *one* of which they used both to sleep with the "Rath" (Florschütz their tutor). The view is beautiful; and the paper is still full of holes from their fencing; and the very same table upon which they were dressed, when little, is there.'[30] The room looks north up the same valley, towards the same hills that the Queen could see from her sitting room; for a few days she shared the view that her husband had known from childhood. Every English visitor since has inquired about the holes in the wallpaper, but they are no longer there. The top of the house is bare and plain, probably much as it has always been.

Albert showed his wife the gardens that he and Ernest had cultivated as children, and the little fort which they had built. It would not be many years before his own children were digging their own little gardens and building a similar fort at Osborne House. Husband and wife walked to the Bathing House and the Fishing Temple. We only know from the souvenir albums what elegant little pavilions these were; today there is no trace of them on the shores of the lake or the banks of the little river that flows below the Rosenau. They took a turn down to the Schweizerei, a real Swiss chalet, which enchanted the Queen with its outside staircase and cattle downstairs.

The Veste from the Rosenau. (Watercolour by Queen Victoria, 1860.)

The Swiss chalet was another idea which found its way to Osborne, but, if you are looking for echoes of Albert's Coburg childhood, you will find them most clearly in the home that he created at Balmoral, where the similarities in atmosphere and appearance are very striking.

'We rose at $\frac{1}{4}$ to 7 – with heavy hearts . . . We took a last look at the dear, peaceful Rosenau, as we drove away'.

27 AUGUST 1845

The Queen loved it all: 'I feel so *at home here*, as if *I had always* been here.'[31] They breakfasted outside in Duke Ernst's favourite spot, and every evening, before the theatre or the levée or the ball, they dined in the Marmorsaal. Afterwards they sat laughing and talking and drinking coffee out on the terrace, where red roses bloom in the summer, and in the distance the brooding silhouette of the Veste crouches on the hilltop above the town. It was all so green and friendly that after only a few days the Queen experienced 'a *feeling* here, which I *can't* describe – a feeling as if *my childhood also* had been spent here'.[32]

We are lucky. We find the Rosenau looking fresh and welcoming, but if we had made this journey a few years ago we would have been sadly disappointed. Throughout the nineteenth century the Rosenau continued to be one of the summer residences of the dukes of Saxe-Coburg and in 1920 it came into the possession of the Coburg State Foundation. After the Second World War it housed refugees and then became an old people's home. In 1972, in a desolate state, it was taken over by the Bavarian Administration of State Palaces, Gardens and Lakes. Between 1985 and 1990 all the colour schemes and gothic decorations were lovingly restored, following the colours hidden away under layers of later paint, and using the watercolours preserved in the Royal Library at Windsor as guides, since these are the best existing records of what the Rosenau looked like in the nineteenth century. The colours of this house, in some places bold to the point of startling (you have to be made of fairly strong stuff to cope with a lapis lazuli drawing room or an emerald green bedroom), contribute to its sophisticated yet friendly feel. Perhaps one of the secrets of the Rosenau's charm is that there is hardly a straight line, and certainly no right-angle, in the entire building, which gives it all a kind of intimacy, though it must have been a nightmare for the designers of the neo-gothic geometric patterns on walls and ceilings.

We left with regret, passing the Swiss chalet, which is now the homestead of a large, prosperous farm. The early frost had gone, and the broad daylight seemed flat and banal.

The day after Albert's birthday Queen Victoria and Prince Albert went on to Gotha. The Queen was in despair at leaving the Rosenau: 'As we drove along I talked it all over with my dearest Albert and we agreed how *charming* it would be if we could live peaceably together at Rosenau; what *liberty* and *happiness*! If I were a *Princess* of England *only*, this would be the case, and *charming* it *would be*. But I must *not* repine. Certainly Ernest has one of *the most enviable* positions imaginable.'[33]

The Road to Reinhardsbrunn and Gotha

Gotha had only come into the possession of the Coburgs in 1826, and is an awkward seventy miles away, across what used to be the Iron Curtain, in the old East Germany. Once more the Queen took to her post chaise, and once more, with her journal on your knee, it is easy to trace her route. As you leave Coburg you can see up on your left the Callenberg, another of Duke Ernst's gothic summer residences, to Queen Victoria 'a fine spot', but today it lurks on its hilltop dilapidated and gloomy and overgrown with trees. Perhaps the restoration it is undergoing at the time of writing will banish its sinister air.

Victoria and Albert stopped in the cheerful little village of Rodach and stepped into the schloss which Albert had known as a shooting lodge; it is still there, now a library. Until 1989 this road virtually came to a dead end a couple of miles further on, as you can see when you come to what was the old East-West border: a few disused but hostile watchtowers and a broad scar running through the woods on the horizon are all that is left. Further on, the countryside still seems closed and empty. Until the border came down there were sometimes as many as five fences; beyond them were minefields – the so-called Death Zone. In the hinterland there was a twenty-kilometre forbidden zone, which only people who lived there could enter freely; visitors needed permits.

Eisenhausen, Hildburghausen: the Queen detailed all the towns along the route, and everywhere the people were dressed in their best and the houses were decorated. It must have been extraordinary to see the queen of a distant country across the sea pass by your door, and people made the most of a unique opportunity. At every town the royal carriage was

Reinhardsbrunn, a hunting lodge on the edge of the Thüringer Wald, built by Albert's father. (Watercolour, left, by Lady Canning, 1845.) After the Rosenau, this was the place which pleased Queen Victoria the most on her trip to Coburg and Gotha.

held up by local clergymen wishing to read her welcoming addresses and by ladies dressed in white and green with wreaths, who in one place 'literally bombarded us with flowers, so that we hardly knew how to save ourselves; and the dirty boys seemed to enjoy it'.[34] Today's traveller, too, is delayed, by detour after detour; every single town in what was East Germany is being dug up, heaps of yellow sand blocking all the roads while new services are being put in.

The Queen was delayed still further in Meiningen, where her party was 'again harangued by the clergyman' and received flowers and verses from young ladies before sitting down with the Duke and Duchess of Meiningen to 'a dinner which (to our despair) lasted terribly long, as we wanted so to get on'.[35] The ducal residence ('like an immense Irish barracks', said Lady Canning[36]) is now a museum. As you leave Meiningen you pass the Schloss Landesburg, 'a very pretty castle of the Duke', says our royal guide, 'which rises from the middle of a plain, with such beautiful meadows which are quite peculiar to Germany'.[37]

You are soon driving through Queen Victoria's favourite kind of scenery: 'beautiful Mountains covered with spruce fir – like Scotland but much more wooded, and we have *no* spruce fir; with valleys and meadows – with little Houses and smoke rising from where the charcoal burners are; so solemn and wild and impressive with such pure cool mountain air'.[38] The Thüringer Wald is still a wild and desolate region, with mists lying in wreaths among the trees, though heavy traffic churns through the blackened valley towns and smoke rises from industrial burners.

It was dark when Queen Victoria reached her destination, a hunting lodge on the edge of the forest, not far from Gotha. Reinhardsbrunn was another of Duke Ernst's neo-gothic fantasies, this one built in 1828 on the site of a Benedictine monastery, and it suited the Queen exactly: 'it is quite lovely; so beautifully and tastefully furnished with poor dear Papa's best taste'.[39] Their rooms were painted with garlands of flowers, and 'all with beautiful parquets and pretty pictures'[40] and balconies on little turrets outside. Downstairs the dining room was 'a fine large room with windows on both sides – our ancestors painted round the ceiling'.[41]

The ancestors are still there in their gothic arches, but to identify them you have to explore some of the obscurer realms of the dynasty, colourful to the point of legend. You will be shown Lewis the Leaper, who founded the monastery in 1085, but you will not see a later scion of the House of Wettin, Albert the Unnatural, who, tiring of his wife, hired a mule-driver to strangle

---

'We drove down a great, but gradual descent, with noble wooded mountains on either side, and valleys, streams, etc., and all the people running after us.'

27 AUGUST 1845

Sitting room of Prince Albert's father, Reinhardsbrunn. (Watercolour by F. Rothbart.) A vanished interior: the painted ceiling is all that remains of what the Queen called 'poor dear Papa's best taste'.

her. The assassin was so overcome by her innocence and virtue that instead of throttling her he let her down from the castle walls in a rope and basket. In the anguish of parting from her child she bit his cheek, drawing blood and leaving him with a scar. He was afterwards known as Frederick the Bitten.[42]

Though the clock on the castle tower striking the hours, and the night watchman on his rounds, kept her awake for some time after she had gone to bed, Queen Victoria confessed that 'After the dear Rosenau, Reinhardsbrunn has pleased me the most of anything, and I am miserable that we could not spend at least a week there.'[43] But they had to go on to Coburg's sister-town, Gotha, for a breathless round (there was barely time to write it all up) of festivals, dancing, processions, church services, introductions and entertainments which mirrored the functions they had already attended. Some evenings, when they were among friends, were obviously fun, as when 'dear

Reinhardsbrunn from the lake, by William Callow.

Albert who sat opposite behaved so ill and laughed so, but it is difficult *not* to do so'.[44] Later so many of her extended family turned up (one night there were ninety-three at dinner) that even the Queen began to complain of the bewildering legions which, rather on the lines of Officers and Other Ranks, she firmly divided up into 'Cousins, Uncles and other Relations'.[45]

Part of one 'enchanting excursion'[46] into the noble forest was much criticized at home; this was the bloody *battue* when for two hours kings and princes shot at deer which had been driven up into an enclosure. The Queen watched, and Albert took part in, the slaughter of some fifty-five animals: 'one gets quite eager and excited', confessed the Queen uneasily, 'fortunately they do not suffer long though it is painful to see how long they run after being wounded … the whole thing was beautifully managed and quite in the old style, but for the sport itself none of the gentlemen like this schlachten [slaughter]'.[47]

All too soon it was the last day – '*too* sad! I feel so sad to go; I can't and won't think of it'.[48]

Queen Victoria did not return to Reinhardsbrunn until 1862, when she spent six weeks here in the first dismal autumn after Albert's death. Today,

The *battue* near Reinhardsbrunn,
with the deer being driven past the
royal shooting party in their pavilion.

there is left only what was out of reach of later plunderers and communist hotel decorators, who all had long arms. On a wet day here it is grim and stifling. The woods of the Thüringer Wald seem to catch the clouds and the rain spills down like the tears of a widowed queen. It drips on the crenellations and the weathervane, falls in circles on the lake and cascades off the dying leaves on the trees. The cracked tongue of the bell sounds the quarter hours marking out the wearisome passage of time, and it is easy to imagine the Queen gazing at the brown lake, with its single swan and dark enclosing trees as she mourned, alone, with a staff of two hundred people to look after her.

The
State Visit
to Paris, 1855

A
Dazzling
Triumph

Since her last visit to the Citizen King, Louis-Philippe, on her way home from Coburg, Queen Victoria had not been to France. Revolution and uprising had in the meantime swept across Europe. One monarch who lost his throne in 1848 was Louis-Philippe. The Second Republic was declared, and three years later its prince president, Louis Napoleon, nephew of Napoleon I, staged a *coup d'état*. ('The whole is like a romantic play!' exclaimed the disagreeably startled Queen across the Channel.[1]) He declared himself Emperor Napoleon III, and while Paris enjoyed the dazzling splendours of the Second Empire England held its breath: it seemed that once again the Napoleonic ogre stalked abroad, and there were even fears of invasion. But instead of going to war against her hereditary enemy, in 1854 England found herself allied with him in the Crimean War against Russia.

In the interests of allied solidarity Napoleon III was invited to Windsor in April 1855. Under the spell of Napoleon's personality all Queen Victoria's distrust melted. The parvenu emperor, experienced man of the world, made up

LEFT: Queen Victoria driving with the Empress Eugénie through the Bois de Boulogne. (Oil painting by Audy.) RIGHT: Arrival of Her Majesty at the Palace of Versailles: this was sightseeing on the grand scale.

Emperor Napoleon III. (Oil painting by Hippolyte Flandrin.) In 1855 England and France were allies against Russia in the Crimea. That Spring, to cement friendly relations between the two countries, the emperor visited Windsor. In August Queen Victoria returned the compliment and went to Paris. The Queen, initially distrustful, remarked after her visit that Napoleon certainly had a most extraordinary power of attracting people to him.

to her in a way she had never quite encountered before, as she tried to explain: 'without *attempting* to do anything in particular to *make* one like him, he had the power of *attaching* those to him who come near him, which is quite *incredible*'.[2] The Queen was indeed, as one acid tongue had it, 'mightily tickled' by the charm of Napoleon III.[3]

To the emperor's attractions were added those of his wife, the Empress Eugénie, a high-born Spaniard. At the time of the marriage, Queen Victoria had heard that she was beautiful, clever, passionate and wild. Such qualities had won Mademoiselle de Montijo an emperor. A queen was no less susceptible. It took only a few days at Windsor for her to become the 'dear Empress'. Her beauty – auburn hair, blue eyes and creamy skin – and graceful ways (her

Empress Eugénie.
(Oil painting by Claude
Marie Dubofe.)
Napoleon's Spanish-born
wife, graceful, chic and
lively, captivated the
whole English royal
family, and she remained
a lifelong friend of the
Queen.

famous curtsey was likened to a flower being bent and then released by the wind) and her well-tempered liveliness were irresistible. She captivated the whole English royal family from the smallest children to Albert himself, who, as a reaction to his father's excesses, was notoriously immune to female beauty. 'I am delighted', wrote the Queen, 'to see how much he likes and admires her, as it is so seldom that I see him do so with any woman.'[4]

The following August Queen Victoria and Prince Albert paid a state visit to Paris in return. They took their two eldest children, Vicky, the Princess Royal, who was fourteen, and Bertie, the Prince of Wales, who was thirteen. They landed at Boulogne on Saturday, 18 August 1855, where they were met by the emperor, most of the town of Boulogne, and forty thousand troops. The

Queen was led ashore by the emperor 'amidst acclamations, salutes, and every sound of joy and respect'.[5] Accompanied by Naopleon III ('who was all kindness and civility'[6]), they proceeded to Paris by train, occupying the imperial saloon.

The Queen looked eagerly out at the new scenery, for some distance 'nothing particular', but after Amiens, 'prettier; many trees, valleys, rivers, small villages, and the fields divided into small partitions'.[7] Refreshments were served on the way on little tables brought in by the emperor's valet, who travelled in the next carriage.

Some five hours later they arrived at the Gare de Chemin de Fer de Strasbourg in Paris and were received into what the Queen called 'the most beautiful and gayest of cities',[8] processing through streets decorated with banners, flags, arches and flowers, hung with welcoming inscriptions and thronged with cheering crowds. It was the first time the city had been visited by an English sovereign since Henry VI had been crowned there as an infant in 1431.

Their ears ringing with the cries of 'Vive la Reine d'Angleterre!', 'Vive l'Empereur!' and 'Vive le Prince Albert!', and with the roar of cannon, bands and drums, they arrived in a blaze of light from lamps and torches at the Palace of Saint Cloud. The Queen felt 'quite bewildered, but enchanted. It was like a fairy tale, and everything so beautiful!'[9]

Triumphal arch at Boulogne, 1855. (Watercolour; artist unknown.)

The Empress Eugénie. (Pencil sketch by Queen Victoria.)

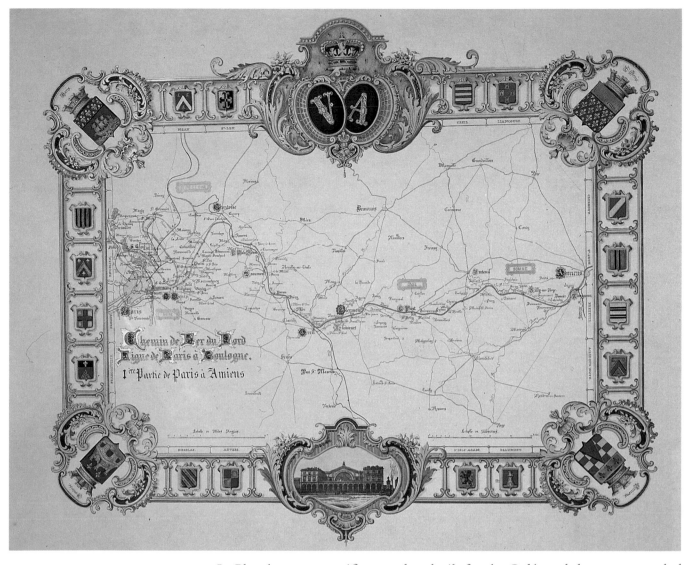

The route taken by the royal train from Paris to Boulogne, showing the first part, from Paris to Amiens.

St Cloud was a magnificent palace built for the Orléans dukes on a wooded escarpment high above the Seine, south-west of Paris. The Queen was all admiration, and could not draw on anything at home for comparison: 'The saloons are all splendid,' she wrote, 'all *en suite* and, as well as the courtyard, staircase, etc., remind me of Brühl. The ceilings are beautifully painted, and the walls hung with Gobelins.'[10] She was equally enchanted with the rooms which had been given over to her, 'furnished with the greatest taste'; the walls were white and gold, the ceilings of her sitting and drawing rooms painted to represent the sky. It was all beautifully and most thoughtfully fitted out, from the paintings which had been brought specially from the Louvre, and the 'charming light green satin furniture', to the gold and glass bottles on the washstand and the 'beautiful *écritoire*' at which to write about it all, with the cool sound of the fountains in her ears. Other noises floated in; the buglers of the Zouaves and the clatter of the Cent Gardes as they rode by under her

The Palace of St Cloud from the Seine, August 1855. (Watercolour by W. Wyld.) This is vanished glory: St Cloud burnt down in 1871, and today only the park remains.

windows. Her bedroom, bathroom and dressing room had a splendid view over Paris, and the other rooms looked over the old-fashioned gardens with orange trees and avenues of beeches.

They would breakfast with the emperor (not the empress, who was pregnant) off Sèvres china, at a round table in a room decorated with three different colours of gold and hung with Gobelins tapestries. But even at breakfast they were surrounded by constant reminders of France's turbulent history, none too safe for kings: one of the tapestries depicted Marie Antoinette, and the very silver they were using, though it dated from the time of the First Empire, had since been engraved with the fleur-de-lis of the Bourbons, no sooner restored than deposed and exiled.

St Cloud was the creation of the brother of Louis XIV, generally known as 'Monsieur', whose first wife, Henrietta of England, died here in 1670. He commissioned Jules-Hardouin Mansart to design the château and Le Nôtre to lay out the park. St Cloud was bought by Marie Antoinette in 1785, and during the Revolution became the property of the state. It was Napoleon's favourite official residence, and in 1810 he married Princess Marie Louise of Austria here

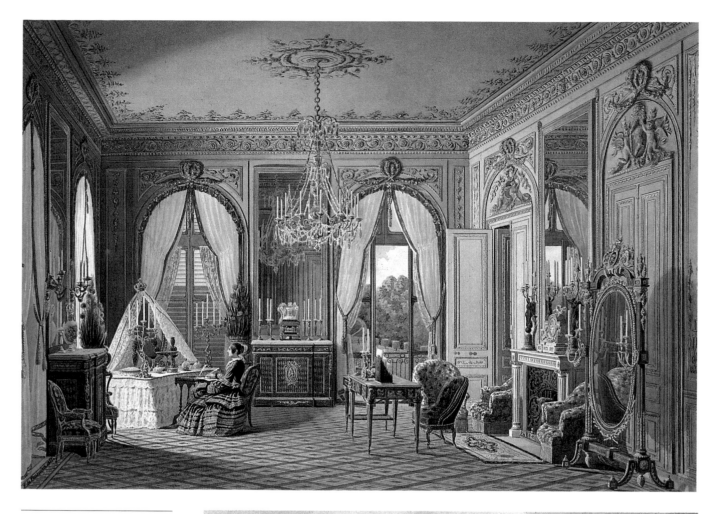

ABOVE: Queen Victoria's dressing room at St Cloud. (Watercolour by F. de Fournier.) RIGHT: Paris from the small garden at St Cloud. (Watercolour by Adolphe Dallemagne.)

(following this civil ceremony with a religious one in the Louvre). It was natural that the Second Empire should follow the precedent of the First, and under Napoleon III St Cloud became one of the five imperial residences.

As the first day of the English visit was Sunday, they took things quietly, merely driving out round the private part of the park of St Cloud and in the Bois de Boulogne, where Albert was most impressed by all the 'improvements' which had been made since the last time he had come to Paris, at the age of fifteen.

On Monday the pace quickened. They drove through the Bois de Boulogne, under the Arc de Triomphe and along the Champs Élysées ('our usual road every day')[11] to the Exposition des Beaux Arts and the Palais de l'Industrie. After lunch at the Élysée ('very pretty, but not neatly fitted up'),[12] the *corps diplomatique* was presented and the emperor then accompanied his guests on a drive round the major sights of Paris.

As ever, the past, in bloody array, was not far off: the Place de la Concorde, where Louis XIV and Marie Antoinette had gone to the guillotine; the grim Conciergerie, where 'l'Autrichienne' had been imprisoned, and which had also for a time held the man now pointing it out to Queen Victoria. She marvelled at the 'Strange, incredible contrast, to be driving with us as Emperor through the streets of the town in triumph!'[13]

They visited that gothic jewel the Sainte Chapelle, 'most exquisitely restored', said the Queen,[14] though modern opinion might beg to differ, and Nôtre Dame – 'the outside is magnificent', conceded Her Majesty, 'but the inside has nothing to admire'.[15] Through the Place de la Bastille, past Napoleon's statue in the Place Vendôme, and so 'home the usual way'.

Coming from the smoke and soot of Dickens's London (his *Little Dorrit* was currently being issued in instalments), Paris seemed white, bright and brilliant. There was much that was new, for under Napoleon III Paris was being transformed: to him and his reign Paris owed the Opéra; the finishing of the galleries which connected the Louvre and the Tuileries; the extension of the Palais de Justice; the widening of the boulevards and the demolition of the higgledy-piggledy medieval streets, which the authorities considered insanitary and too easy for the popu-lace to defend against regular troops.

Sketches by Queen Victoria at St Cloud. Busy as she was with sights and entertainments, the Queen still found time to observe and record.

ABOVE: Queen and
Empress drive, Prince and
Emperor ride. BELOW:
Queen Victoria at the
Queen's House, Petit
Trianon, 20 August 1855.
(Watercolour by Karl
Girardet.)

The next day they paid what the Queen called a 'most interesting, instructive, and melancholy'[16] visit to Versailles, where the grandeur of the Sun King had reached its zenith. Queen Victoria's account of the great palace makes curious reading for us, for at one moment in the chapel she said, 'one can well imagine Louis XIV present', and we realize that she was using the same imaginative process as we were in envisaging her here. Versailles made a deep impression on her, 'and seemed to bring back all the French history, with its many strange and dark events to our mind. And to see all this with the Emperor was even more striking.'[17]

Queen Victoria's sightseeing took an odd turn when she arrived at the Grand Trianon, and was shown the bed which had been prepared for her by Louis-Philippe when he had expected her to visit Paris. They drove through the gardens, 'full of brilliant flowers, including a number of gladioli, which they put into the gardens in large quantities here, and which enliven the landscape very greatly',[18] to the Petit Trianon, redolent as nowhere else of the spirit of Marie Antoinette.

They stopped for luncheon in the largest of the cottages of the Hameau, the make-believe village where 'the poor unhappy Queen', Marie Antoinette, had

played at being a rustic. Queen Victoria, a great preserver of souvenirs herself, noted with approval how well looked after it all was, and how the emperor was leaving everything in its place.

From one stage set to another: in the evening they drove into Paris to the Grand Opéra in Rue Lepelletier for a concert of opera extracts and ballet. Although it was all very grand, with the royal box arranged 'in the centre of the house, as when we go to the Opera in state',[19] and although they received a 'hearty reception' from the crowded audience, the evening was not a complete success. For a start both Queen and empress *and* another princess were all dressed alike, in white, with diamond and emerald jewellery; the heat was 'quite fearful', and the first performance 'I did not think a very happy arrangement', while the second was 'too long'. What the Queen really enjoyed was the last item, wherein 'a view of Windsor, with the Emperor's arrival, appeared, and *God Save the Queen* was sung splendidly, and most enthusiastically cheered'.[20] They drove back to St Cloud after midnight, the emperor and Albert singing German songs.

Paris in 1855 was following the example set by London in 1851 and was staging its own Great Exhibition. The earlier event at the Crystal Palace had been truly innovative. Albert had been closely involved, and it had finally brought him the public recognition which the Queen had always known was his due. By 1855 these shows of art and technology were no longer a novelty for the Queen, who recognized some of the items on display, having already seen them in London, and confined her purchases to '*one* small object'.

There was, however, one place in Paris that ignited the spark of envy in her bosom: the palace of the Tuileries, Catherine de Medici's great Renaissance pile (built on the site of tile-kilns, hence the name). Grand as it was, the Tuileries had a violent history, and the Paris mob had a habit of sacking it: first in 1789 (keeping the doomed family of Louis XVI and Marie Antoinette virtual prisoners there); they then threw out Charles X in 1830 and Louis-Philippe in 1848. This history of royal evictions might have made the emperor think twice about living there, but the palace had been Napoleon I's principal residence and so had powerful Napoleonic associations. After what the Queen called the 'horrors' of 1848 Napoleon III had the Tuileries completely redecorated and made it his official residence in Paris. When she saw the state rooms the Queen declared 'everything is on such a large scale and so truly regal, that it makes me quite jealous and unhappy that our great country and particularly our great metropolis, should be devoid of all this'.[21] And yet, from these very windows she could see the obelisk in the Place de la Concorde which marked the spot where Louis XVI, Marie Antoinette and so many others were guillotined. Victoria, merely a visiting queen, could look upon it and indulge in 'what sad reflections'; the Emperor of the French felt it spoilt the view.

It was typical of the Queen that, in the midst of all the public acclaim and official glitter, she should wish to drive incognito round the city. The emperor was 'much amused' and arranged where they should go. Heavily veiled, she set out with Albert, who sat well back. 'Just as we were going through the gates the curious crowd looked very much into the carriage, which was stopped for a moment, and we felt very foolish.'[22] But they got away safely and much enjoyed a long drive, the Queen fascinated by the street life, 'the quantities of people and soldiers in bright colours, *marchands de coco* etc.; the people sitting and drinking before the houses, all so foreign and southern looking to my eyes and *so* gay'.[23] But the best part about the whole expedition was that they got back to the Tuileries safely 'without being known'.

Not surprisingly, the Queen rested when she got back to St Cloud: ahead of her she still had a dinner with eighty guests and an evening at the theatre. She was thriving on it all, though, whereas Albert was not: late nights and the social whirl had never suited him. The Queen, however, did make some concessions to the demands of her heavy schedule, as when going round the Louvre the next day, 'unfortunately very, very hurriedly' (but still a marathon three and a half hours), she allowed herself to be wheeled around in a little chair.

At a quiet moment between engagements, as she sat writing in the empress's room in the Tuileries, its sombre, inescapable history pressed in upon her again: 'All so gay – the people cheering the Emperor as he walked up and down in the little garden – and yet how recently has blood flowed and a whole dynasty been swept away. How uncertain is everything still!'[24]

She was a little vague about how many people had been invited to the ball in the Hôtel de Ville that evening – seven or nine thousand, she supposed. Her toilette for the occasion somehow sums her up: her white net dress was embroidered with gold and trimmed with red geraniums, and she wore her diamond diadem set with the famous Koh-i-noor. Parisians, and Queen Victoria's biographers, have never quite got over the red geraniums.

The royal party ascended a staircase decorated with flags, emblems, flowers, a fountain and two statues representing France and England, danced one ceremonious quadrille (how different from the 'incessant' dancing at Coburg) and toured the crowded salons. The Hôtel de Ville had had every bit as exciting and unsettling a history as the Tuileries: 'This occasion will erase all sad memories', suggested the emperor hopefully.

Review in the Champ de
Mars, 24 August 1855.
(Watercolour by
R. Thomas.) The Queen
took a great interest in the
French troops, comrades
of those fighting
alongside her own in the
Crimea.

So far Queen Victoria had paid her respects to the arts and to modern
industry (she made several visits to different sections of the Exhibition), had
dwelt on the history of the kings of France and had accepted the invitation of
the mayor of Paris to his ball; now it was the turn of the military.

The weather grew hotter and heavier by the day. With large drops of rain
spitting out of a threatening sky, the Queen attended a review on the Champ de
Mars of some thirty or forty thousand troops. She always had an expert eye for
a good turn-out and military drill. She sat on the balcony of the École Militaire
and watched them all march past, glad to see these brave comrades-in-arms of
her own troops.

In what the Queen called 'perhaps the most important act of all in this
interesting and eventful time'[25] they paid homage to the greatest soldier of
them all, visiting the unfinished tomb of Napoleon in the Invalides. 'I stood, at
the arm of Napoleon III his nephew, before the coffin of our bitterest foe, I, the
granddaughter of that King who most vigorously opposed him, and this very
nephew, who bears his name, being my nearest and dearest ally!'[26] The Queen
put her hand on the shoulder of the Prince of Wales and made him kneel. A
thunderclap sounded overhead and the rainstorm finally broke.

The princely entertainments continued with a meet of the royal pack of hounds at the hunting lodge, La Muette, which was situated in the forest of St Germain, not far from the old Palace of St Germain, neglected and ruinous, where James II of England had died. They reached their peak with a ball at Versailles, 'which', wrote the Queen, 'was quite one of the finest and most magnificent sights we have ever witnessed. There had not been a ball at Versailles since the time of Louis XVI, and the design of this one had been taken from a fête given by Louis XV.'[27]

The 26 August was Albert's birthday: 'this *dearest* of days was not ushered in as usual, nor spent as I could have wished, but my dear Albert was pleased, and it was spent with those who do appreciate him as they ought'.[28] The Queen's presents were laid out for him on a table surrounded by a wreath, and consisted of 'a very fine bronze of the celebrated Belgian group "*Le Lion amoureux*," and some pretty little Alliance and Crimean studs, the third button having a blank, I hope for Sevastopol'.[29]

The visit to Paris concluded with the traditional exchange of extravagant presents, the Emperor Napoleon insisting that the Queen take home with her the gold and glass tumblers and bottles with her initials on them which had been generously provided on her washstand. Thereafter they stood on her dressing table at Windsor.

They took leave of the empress in Paris (she and Vicky were both in tears) and the emperor accompanied his visitors on the train to Boulogne and saw them on board the royal yacht. The Queen looked over the side of the ship as she heard the splash of the oars of his barge, which was lit by the moon and by all the blue lights of the yacht, and reflected on his enigmatic personality: 'His society is particularly agreeable and pleasant; there is something fascinating, melancholy, and engaging, which draws you to him in spite of any *prévention* you may have against him.'[30] The state visit had been a personal and diplomatic success.

Back home again, the Queen felt 'very excited' (a sensation she disliked) and 'unable to do anything but talk all day of everything we had seen and done'.[31] Two days later her journal entry concluded quietly: 'We dined alone and were occupied in arranging and sorting out prints and views of Paris, and in cutting out the very good woodcuts from the Illustrated News, for our Journey Album.'[32] When we came across a similar large folder in the Royal Library containing woodcuts of this visit, it was easy to imagine the two of them together poring over a volume like it and reliving the experiences of those heady few days.

FOLLOWING PAGE: Queen Victoria at the tomb of Napoleon I. (Oil painting by E. M. Ward.) She was quite overcome by the drama of the occasion: 'I, the granddaughter of that King who most vigorously opposed him, and this very nephew, who bears his name, being my nearest and dearest ally!'

CHAPTER FIVE

The Delightful Fortnight, Potsdam, 1858

The Gothic Bijou

'In response to a tentative request for help and the promise of three autographs, a small group of forestry workers transformed the edge of the wood at Babelsberg into a stage set for a portrait shot. In some astonishment but with a wonderful willingness they set to work with steel hawsers to relocate the portion of the forest on which I sit.'

'Were it not for you, dear child, nothing would make me undertake this long, and I fear very fatiguing journey.'[1] Queen Victoria was put out, on two counts. Her daughter Vicky, who had married Prince Frederick William of Prussia barely six months earlier, was already expecting a child. The Queen had hoped that her eighteen-year-old daughter would not get 'caught', as she put it, so early in her marriage, and now it meant that the princess, carrying a possible heir to the Prussian throne, would not be allowed to travel. In order to see her daughter Queen Victoria must make the long, dull journey all the way to Berlin.

Even though Victoria and Albert travelled by train the whole way, the journey was still an endurance test on account not only of the distances but also of the exhausting welcomes, which the Queen had feared.

The royal yacht *Victoria and Albert* left Gravesend on the morning of 10 August 1858, made the mouth of the Scheldt by the evening and anchored off Flushing for the night. The next morning the royal couple landed at Antwerp. They were conveyed to the station in carriages belonging to Uncle Leopold, who accompanied them for part of the way. At Aix-la-Chapelle they were welcomed into Prussian territory by the Prince of Prussia, and they broke their journey at Düsseldorf where they dined at the Jägerhof. 'The house is old', wrote the Queen dismissively (it was built in 1772), 'and only has one large room'. The Jägerhof has a chequered history: sacked by French Revolutionary troops in 1796, it was gutted by bombs in 1943 and rebuilt, and today it houses a museum devoted to Goethe. After dinner the Queen and Prince 'stepped onto the balcony to look at the beautiful illuminations, all up the avenue transparent paper lamps, and some like baskets of flowers, also splendid red and blue lights, which had the most charming effect. We drove back to the inn, as we came, through dense, cheering crowds, lights and fireworks everywhere, really the

The Jägerhof in Düsseldorf (watercolour by August Becker), where the Queen broke her journey to Berlin in 1858. Long, hot train journeys and exhausting welcomes at stopping places tested the Queen's powers of endurance.

prettiest I have ever seen, and so tastefully arranged. All was the spontaneous act of the Artists and the inhabitants.'[2]

They spent the night at the Breidenbacherhof, a hotel opened by an entrepreneur, William Breidenbach, during the Napoleonic Wars. From its earliest days it housed the rich and famous, and Europe's royalty stayed there before Queen Victoria graced its neo-classical portals, as they still do today. In the 1940s it suffered as badly as the rest of Düsseldorf from war damage. It rose anew from the rubble to become once again the haunt of the rich and elegant, in an area of the city where great banks rub shoulders with shops to tempt the people who have everything: mink-lined raincoats and crocodile suitcases are on display, along with gold and diamonds on female torsos of polished marble. 'A fearfully hot night', complained Queen Victoria, 'rooms so stuffy, and much noise in the street.'[3]

They were up again at six and on their way by seven. The Queen was sorely tried: 'the heat and dust became almost unbearable'.[4] They had a wearisome

Potsdam from the
Wilhelms-Bank in the
park of Babelsberg.
(Watercolour by
C. Graeb.) Today, the
trees have grown up so
that only the tip of the
tower on the right is
visible.

halt in Hanover, where the King and Queen of Hanover took them to
Herrenhausen, 'a curious low, old wooden house, with wings and green
shutters',[5] and a 'French garden and splendid orange trees, fountains, statues,
etc., quite in the style of Versailles'.[6] The famous gardens were mainly the
creation of the Electress Sophia, a link in the chain of succession to the English
throne: she was the last Protestant Stuart, and if she had not died in this garden
in 1714 she would have become Queen of England. Three months later,
incidentally while he was here, her son became George I. Today the gardens are
beautifully restored, but all that remains of the rococo palace, demolished by
allied bombs in 1943, is a flat, green lawn.

The heat, the luncheon, the stiff conversation, the tour of the palace and
gardens, the lengthy presentations and the tour round the town delayed the
travellers so badly that they left Hanover an hour and a half behind schedule:
'Dreadful,' cried the Queen. 'Continued our journey in the most awful heat
and dust, I with a racking headache.'[7]

'Here on the platform stood our darling child with a nosegay in her hand and stepped into our saloon. Warm was the embrace, as she clasped me in her arms, so much to say, to ask, to tell . . .'

12 AUGUST 1859

There was not even any decent scenery to take her mind off her misery, 'nothing but a flat ugly country'.[8] The sandy plains of Prussia are extraordinarily anonymous: wheat fields broken only by stands of fir trees and silver birch continue for mile after mile, hour after hour, with an occasional pair of deer frozen like statues, or distant farm machinery moving in slow motion. The longer you travel the less you feel you are getting anywhere.

'It became gradually dark', said the Queen, 'and the time seemed very long as we gradually approached nearer the end of our journey.' Then there at last was her daughter boarding the train with a posy of flowers in her hand. 'Warm was the embrace, as she clasped me in her arms. So much to say, to ask, to tell, the dear child still so unaltered, looking well and quite our *old* Vicky.'[9]

In another few moments they were at Potsdam. Seventeen miles southwest of Berlin, Potsdam had once been a small market town in a pleasant wooded region of interconnecting lakes and waterways. In the seventeenth century it had caught the fancy of the Great Elector and he had built himself a summer palace there. Later princes, in particular Frederick the Great (1712–86), each added their own flights of fancy to its architectural glories, and Potsdam became known as the Prussian Versailles. Every summer all the Prussian royal family (a large and quarrelsome tribe) left their establishments in Berlin and spent the hottest months among the woods and parks close to the cool waters of the lakes. When the railways came several stations were conveniently sited for royal use. At Potsdam station, where a band and a guard of honour 'of most enormously tall Guardsmen, wearing pointed caps' awaited them, Queen Victoria and Prince Albert got into open carriages to be driven to one of the very newest of the palaces, Schloss Babelsberg.

On a dark autumn day, more than one hundred and thirty years later, we are driving through the once elegant suburbs which sprang up in the vicinity of the royal palaces. From the end of the Second World War until 1989 Potsdam lay in East Germany. A cold wind is blowing, the sky is dull and leaden, and it is as though a film of grey has settled over everything, over the shabby houses and wet cobbled streets, over the branches of the trees still hung with a few tatty leaves and the hunched shoulders of the pedestrians shuffling along the broken pavements. We lose our way among the featureless streets, where there are no street signs. The golden rectangle of an occasional new shop window sends out an encouraging glow of consumerism, but otherwise this place is as thick with the cobwebs of the past as Miss Havisham's dusty wedding breakfast in Charles Dickens's *Great Expectations*.

We have a map, pre-1989, which shows the royal palaces in red and their

Schloss Babelsberg by C. Graeb, elegantly situated above the Havel, with the Glienicke Bridge in the distance. Its neo-gothic architecture suited the Queen's taste exactly; she considered it quite the most 'livable' of all the palaces in Potsdam.

surrounding parks in pale, summery green. Babelsberg, in red, surrounded by a good deal of green, is marked in the top right-hand corner, close to a stretch of blue water, but beyond it is a grey blank where the Berlin Wall shut off the western sector of the city. The grey blank effectively puts castle and park on the rim of a flat earth: beyond the rim, says the map, is a cultural void and it might as well not exist.

We turn up a wide, straight street which becomes an avenue. We are not far now from the grey blank on the map, and we have entered what was so recently the forbidden zone. We turn in past a little dilapidated gothic gatehouse and wind along a sandy track. Through the trees many greyish-yellow 'irregular turrets, towers and steps'[10] come into view, instantly familiar from the sunlit watercolours in the Royal Library at Windsor. This is Schloss Babelsberg, elegantly situated but looking rather forlorn now among its overgrown ornamental trees, and the yellowish towers do not suggest romantic castles so much as early English factories.

In the beautiful park designed by Lenné (whose work we saw at Brühl), there is no one about except a single gardener, laying new marble chips round a dried up fountain on the terrace. In front of the castle open ground falls away to the shore of the lake, the Havel; on the other side of the water is the Glienicke Bridge, which once spanned the gulf between East and West and was made famous, or notorious, by exchanges of spies during the Cold War.

Babelsberg was a summer palace and its entrance is through a cool, underground passage tiled in blue and white like the summer apartments at Brühl. It was eleven o'clock at night before Queen Victoria finally entered this 'small castle, with halls, terraces, flowers, etc., and most tasteful, curious small staircases'.[11]

At first sight it seems odd that she should call it small, but when you look at it closely you see that it is artfully designed to look much larger than it really is. It was an entirely new building, started in 1834, after plans drawn up by none other than Karl Friedrich Schinkel; having seen Stolzenfels, the Ehrenburg and the Rosenau, no wonder this feels familiar. It belonged to Vicky's father-in-law (we met him, with his muttonchop whiskers, hanging next to his brother, the King of Prussia, at Stolzenfels) and had been started for him when he was plain Prince William of Prussia. When he became crown prince, however, and felt that he needed a more splendid residence, the plans were enlarged by Ludwig Persius and Heinrich Strack.

Prince William did not enjoy the same domestic bliss as his brother, the king. As a young man he had been desperately in love with a noble beauty, but because she was not royal he had not been allowed to marry her. Instead, he had done his duty and married Princess Augusta of Saxe-Weimar. It was a stormy relationship. It was said that he insisted his wife use a tea service which had once belonged to his mother. She hated it, and contrived to drop most of the cups.

Staying in one place for so long, the Queen had more time than on previous trips abroad to work up her sketches: TOP LEFT: the Marmorpalais; TOP RIGHT AND BOTTOM; Glienicke Bridge.

He had the Royal Berlin Porcelain Company copy the entire set and presented it to her on her next birthday.

The prince and princess, as Queen Victoria referred to them, had lent her Babelsberg for her visit. 'The Princess and Vicky took us to our rooms, which are very comfortable . . . Took off my bonnet and tidied myself a little, then went below where we supped'.[12]

The next morning, looking out on a view of water, woods and lakeside palaces, the Queen described her rooms in more detail:

> I have a pretty, small dressing-room, with a balcony, and near it our bedroom (the Princess's own room) then up steps, a fine large room, like a lantern (the Prince's room) with a nice large writing table, at which I am writing, and which I use as my sitting room . . . Albert's dressing and sitting rooms are a few steps down, opening on to the gallery by which one gets to Vicky's rooms. From this gallery one looks down upon two splendid rooms, the Dining and Ball rooms, which are in fact high Gothic Halls.[13]

They breakfasted 'in the Library, the last of the suite of smaller rooms below, of which there are four'.[14] You can imagine the life and the bustle. There would have been all the endless questions and answers, the laughter and the vibrant talk of people who are glad to see one another after time spent apart.

The Queen loved Babelsberg, this 'Gothic "bijou" – full of furniture, flowers, and creepers (so prettily arranged around screens) lamps and pictures'.[15] Today, as you enter these same downstairs rooms, your head is full of the Queen's descriptions. The remembered riches of Stolzenfels and Brühl keep you expectant of finding something else: surely there must be more to it than this? Where are the gothic screens and the pretty creepers, the flowers, the lamps and the pictures, the desks and little button-backed seats? All gone, swept away by time and war, leaving bare rooms; only the painted designs on the walls are left, the airy, spacious proportions and the fine views. The rooms contain only a small collection of topographical paintings, a few little gothic chairs as finicky as cobwebs, and memorabilia of the Prussian royal family – ink stands, faded photographs and campaigning souvenirs – spread out in glass cases for all to see. In the library our attention is drawn to the white gothic plasterwork ceiling, apparently inspired by the ceiling in the choir of St George's Chapel at Windsor. It is about all there is to see, except for the lantern, which was a present from Queen Victoria and Prince Albert, hanging at a depressed angle in the decaying glass porch. It is only next door that we find anything familiar, for here we step through into the enchanted ballroom,

'I was fascinated by the Glienicke Bridge as it is today, and stopped to paint it while we were on our travels. Its cold iron arches still seem haunted by the ghosts of fear and suspicion from the long years when it was the meeting point of East and West.'

The ballroom at Babelsberg, as it was in the 1850s (watercolour, above, by C. Graeb) when it was used as a dining room, and as it is today, a miraculous survival when so much else that was here has been swept away.

Summer in Potsdam, long ago, when the breezy arcades of Babelsberg were cool and inviting. (Watercolour by C. Graeb.)

which we saw in the great scarlet album marked Berlin. The towering gothic pillars still support the high, blue ceiling, with its riot of vegetation and putti playing musical instruments among the spandrels; even the blue velvet chairs with lions' heads on the arms are still there – a miraculous survival since the rest of the castle is so empty. Set unobtrusively into the pillars are central heating vents with gothic grilles: Babelsberg was comfortable make-believe.

The ballroom is open to the public but the other 'high Gothic Hall', the dining room, is not. It is still being used by the Brandenburg State Research Office for Pre- and Early History, as are the rooms upstairs where Queen Victoria stayed. Through a crack in the door we glimpse only a shining wooden floor and a chandelier. The other features of the hall – fretwork throne, carved overmantel, gallery and assorted tudor-style trappings – if they still exist, are dark and invisible.

'After breakfast and talking', wrote Queen Victoria, 'we fetched our hats

and walked about in the grounds but the heat was quite sickening. Charming walks under trees, and fountains on all the terraces.'[16] A good place to sit on such a day would have been on the gothic seats in the shady arcades, which catch the slightest breeze, with the soothing trickle of a nearby fountain to create an illusion of coolness. The Queen had a painting of it by Graeb at Windsor, but it takes us a while here among the battered archways to work out why present reality does not match the allure of the painting; then we realize that half the arcades no longer exist – they had become so dangerous that they were demolished early this century.

From here we have a good view down to the lake, which offered opportunities for charming excursions. One evening a small steamer, with sailors dressed as Russians, took the royal party along the Havel to the Pfaueninsel, or Peacock Island. Here there was 'a small curious old building furnished in an old-fashioned way',[17] which may well have been the little folly

'Nothing could exceed
the kind and markedly
friendly manner, in
which we have been
received everywhere. It
is very striking, as the
visit has been considered
as quite private and
unofficial'.

23 AUGUST 1858

ordered by Frederick William II in 1793 ('splendid place for fantasy castle', he is reported to have said; 'have something gothic built immediately'). A large gathering of royalty took tea in the Palm House:

> sitting there till half past seven, a band playing. The evening was warm, still, and beautiful, and we were a very merry party. At half past eight we all (except the Princess, who feared the night air) re-embarked and had a very pleasant steam back by moonlight, as we approached Glienicke, illuminations (red and blue lights) began and Babelsberg was beautifully lit up. We got close enough to step on shore, at the same place where we had got into the boats, walking up some steps which were entirely illuminated by coloured lamps and 'lampions', the whole way to the Schloss. There were besides festoons of small lamps on the ground, the whole looking quite fairylike.[18]

We find it difficult to imagine a balmy evening at Babelsberg, even though our sullen day has suddenly turned fine; the sun stays out while we explore and think about the past, imagining Queen Victoria and Prince Albert spending a fortnight here with their daughter. She was Albert's favourite child and the one most like him. Here in Prussia she had a loving husband and a happy marriage, but she was generally disliked and mistrusted for the same reason as he was unpopular in England, simply for being foreign. Vicky was to have a hard time of it in Prussia.

In the park, where work is going on to open up many of the viewpoints and vistas designed by Lenné, we take a last look at the gothic 'bijou'. Just as we decide it is time to go, as though some accompanying spirit is saying goodbye, the bleak sun goes in and a cold wind whistles down from the north-east, sending a flurry of leaves across the ride, and making us hurry to the car.

Out walking one morning with Vicky, the Queen passed 'the monument close to the house (St Michael destroying the dragon) given the Prince by the King, in remembrance of the Baden campaign'. (Journal, 18 August 1858.) In 1848 the Prince of Prussia, now Vicky's father-in-law, had quelled the dragon of revolution with particular ferocity.

The Palaces of Sans Souci

'It may readily be supposed that guests of such distinction would be shown everything that was of interest in and around Potsdam.' So wrote a contemporary journalist and, eager to see everything of interest ourselves, we zoom off past the shabby mansions and through the potholed streets, across a wide bridge, the Lange Brücke, only to find ourselves stuck in the traffic. Eastern road systems have not been designed to cope with western traffic.

We have with us copies of the watercolours from the souvenir albums, just ordinary photographs the size of postcards, and we have grown used to comparing views of then and now, to being able to stand where the artist stood so many years ago, to seeing what he saw and trying to interpret it as he did. At Brühl, at Stolzenfels, at Coburg, even at dilapidated Babelsberg, these postcards from the past have brought the Queen's journeys alive. At the moment, on the top of the bundle of Potsdam views we have a lively scene which for many years masqueraded as a picture of a review at Aldershot, when in fact it shows Queen Victoria on 17 August 1858 at a review in the Lustgarten in front of the Potsdamer Schloss. This palace, built between 1660 and 1701, launched Potsdam as a royal playground. The Queen summed it up in passing as 'enormous, and in the style of Louis xivth and xvth',[19] with some fine rooms, but her attention that morning was concentrated on Albert riding 'a fine grey horse of Fritz's', 'endless Generals', and about four thousand soldiers marching past 'in very quick time, with that peculiar step, throwing the leg out and stamping, but it is not as disagreeable "en masse" as it is singly'.[20]

The lights have turned green but we are still stuck. They turn red again. Ahead of us is the awkward pepperpot dome of the Nikolaikirche, which has characterized the skyline of Potsdam since 1845, and crammed in next to it, as though trying to shoulder it out of the way, is a hideous cream and white shoebox building. In front is a tangle of roads, tramlines and electricity wires and, somewhere in the middle of these eyesores, a long, low building with stout pillars, telltale eighteenth-century windows and powerful stone horses prancing over the porticoes. The lights are amber. Horses mean stables, and stables like these in royal Potsdam can only mean a palace, and isn't there something faintly familiar about these? The lights go green again, and suddenly the pieces of a puzzle that is now so incomplete and damaged as to be almost unrecognizable fall into place. With a thrill of discovery and horror we realize that these are the horses on the building depicted behind the Queen's carriage in the picture of the Lustgarten. This architectural mess in front of us, and this wide and desolate space, is the site of the Potsdamer Schloss which was

Queen Victoria at a review in the Lustgarten, outside the Potsdamer Schloss, 17 August 1858. (Watercolour by G. H. Thomas.) As we drove through this wide space we barely recognized where we were, so shattered and mangled are the pieces of the puzzle.

destroyed in the bombardment of 14 April 1945. As we at last move on we are actually driving through the picture, right past the spot where the Queen's carriage stood. The whole car is a buzz of excitement and the horses seem to dance along the stable rooftop.

'The roads very rough',[21] remarked Queen Victoria when she drove through the town; here at least not much has changed. We judder along over the cobblestones and it is not long before we stop beside a large heap of yellow sand at the entrance to Potsdam's most famous building, Sans Souci.

Sans Souci, 'Free of Care': Frederick the Great was no different from many another monarch in wanting a quiet place where he could escape the cares of state. In 1744 he planted a terraced vineyard outside the town of Potsdam, on the southern slope of a low eminence called Desert Hill. The following year he began to build a miniature palace retreat on the uppermost terrace.

As we approach Sans Souci from the town we glimpse its columns above us and catch sight of the back of the building, which faces over the terraces. We pick our way through the sand heaps and the workmen laying new cobblestones and enter a forecourt encircled by a colonnade. As you stand on

the gravel outside the entrance your eye is caught by a ruin and some lonely columns on a hill on the horizon. Not another direct hit, left unrepaired for fifty years? No, it is a folly, the Ruinenberg (grandiosely translated as the Mount of Ruins), designed in the eighteenth century to remind the king of the transience of all things. In the drab, scarred environs of the town of Potsdam, such deliberate ruins seem rather unnecessary now.

We turn back towards Frederick the Great's escape. There are no arms or crests to tell you who lived here for this was, above all, a private place. Inside, the single-storey building is a far cry from the painted gothic of 'poor dear Papa', or the gothic 'bijou' at Babelsberg. We are back in the world of marble pillars, gilded acanthus leaves and cloud-borne cupids scattering flowers. We pass along a narrow hall lined with statues, where Frederick the Great's collection of paintings by Watteau hung until they vanished in the Second World War. A wide-beamed woman in overalls is tickling a statue of Bacchus with a duster, and everywhere her colleagues are running electric polishers over the lustrous parquet. The whole carefully tended palace, with all its splendid and fanciful flourishes, gleams and sparkles.

Gilded grapevines dangle everywhere, and on the walls the gilded panels are ribbed like the patterns left in sand by waves. We penetrate a warren of

LEFT: Rococo Sans Souci (meaning without cares), overgrown with nineteenth-century romanticism. (Watercolour by C. Graeb.) RIGHT: The terraces today.

passages, peer into a circular library with a pretty pink and blue ceiling and a huge fireplace which cries out for a roaring fire, and pass through a drawing room under the signs of the zodiac. Beyond is a concert room where a spider spins her web of gold overhead and golden hounds give chase across the ceiling; gilded sunflowers hang in heavy garlands across mirrors and gilded gourds grow and swell on doors. The concert room is filled with music and we look around for the musicians or a sound system, but it is coming from a slim-waisted clock which stands on a commode between exquisite, bandy-legged

chairs upholstered in their original soft red silk damask. In the so-called Voltaire room, like feverish hallucinations, the custard-yellow walls are covered with gaudy three-dimensional parrots, monkeys and storks, and pomegranates and roses riot across the ceiling. The centre of the palace is the oval hall, whose tall windows even on a dull day allow pale light to come pouring in onto marble columns and the teasing rococo figures who look down at us from a great height. One carving depicts a cupid who is about to take a hammer to a half-finished column while a goddess raises a horrified hand to stop him.

None of it cut any ice with Queen Victoria. In her opinion Sans Souci was 'very low dark damp and cheerless'.[22] Now, in an age which takes it for granted that the works of the eighteenth century are to be admired, this seems an astonishing reaction, but her taste was in line with her contemporaries who also thought it 'low, and not a handsome building'.[23] As one of them firmly put it, 'Sans Souci is not interesting for architectural beauty, but because Frederick the Great lived in it'.[24]

More to the Queen's taste were the 'lovely' terraces outside, where she thought 'the flat grave stones of Frederick the Great's dogs, are very interesting with their inscriptions & all the names engraved. It is said that he wished himself to be buried there.'[25] He did, but his wishes were not fulfilled until 17 August 1991, the two hundred and fifth anniversary of his death, when his remains were finally brought here, and now lie under a slab not much bigger than the stones which mark the graves of his whippets. Beside his tomb is a statue of Flora, the goddess of flowers, boxed into a little wooden hut to preserve her from winter frosts, and as we stand at the top of the famous terraces, which are screened by glass panels to protect the replanted grapevines and fig trees, we see that the statues in the great park are all being boxed in.

Sans Souci occupies only one corner of the large landscaped park which bears its name. The place is dotted with villas and follies reflecting whatever fantasy seized the royal builders' imagination, from a Chinese teahouse to Roman baths. In 1990 this magnificent landscape designed by Lenné was put on the World Heritage List, and we are seeing it all at a time of transformation, part mouldering with the effects of neglect and pollution, part shining with new gold.

By far the largest building at Sans Souci is one of the oldest, known as the Neues Palais, or New Palace, at the far end of the park. Driving to it one 'splendid' evening, the Queen was reminded of Versailles.[26] One can imagine mother and daughter remembering all the excitement of their visit to Paris as they drove comfortably along in Vicky's 'turn-out', which, approved Mama, 'is very pretty, 4 black horses with two postillions and outriders, the carriage a very open, easy barouche, with a footman and "Jäger" [outdoor servant] behind'.[27]

The Neues Palais is also the work of Frederick the Great, built between 1763 and 1769 to prove to the world that he still had something left after fighting the Seven Years' War. He never really lived there, preferring Sans

Under the central dome of Sans Souci is the marble hall. Queen Victoria confined her comments here to the minimum: 'Frederick the Great built the Schloss and died there. It is very low, dark, damp and cheerless.'

Souci. Queen Victoria came here through the park but we approached it from outside, glimpsing beyond a rusty fence and huge, blackened colonnades a soaring copper dome surmounted by the Three Graces holding up a crown. All along the top of a dusty pink façade that stretches from horizon to horizon we can make out a standing army of grimy statues. We lose sight of the palace again as we drive on further and turn in at a flimsy gate. Two stately buildings, with sweeping steps, pillars, cupolas, obelisks and all the other grand appurtenances of state, come into view. But these buildings, called the Communs, are only the kitchens – surely the grandest and most impractical in the world – several hundred yards away across a sandy forecourt from the towering cliff-face of the palace itself. We drive on and stop in front of the entrance, under the copper dome. As though Frederick had not bragged enough in conceiving a palace on such a scale, he had all the window frames of this central section gilded on the outside.

Decayed majesty and decrepit beauty are apparent everywhere. Far above us the statues along the rooftop lean precariously out, each enveloped in a blackened crust. Looking across to the Communs, we see that one has lost its

dome and the other is apparently supported by extremely ancient scaffolding. During the war a bomb hit the colonnade (the gap is still there), and sizeable trees now flourish along the top, which used to be lined with statues; these figures have been taken down, and stand in concerned little groups as if discussing the large blue tarpaulins nearby which presumably cover up other sections of the fallen buildings.

When Queen Victoria swept through the Neues Palais she looked at it from the viewpoint of someone who might actually live in it: 'Endless suites of apartments, – 2 sets of State Rooms, very splendidly furnished, and no end of living rooms, all fine and lofty, but anything but cheerful . . . We saw the room downstairs, in which Fritz was born, the Prince and Princess having had to live there in 31, during the time the cholera was so bad at Berlin.' But in spite of these interesting family associations, and the fact that Vicky was 'very partial to the Neues Palais' (she was to live there for many years), Queen Victoria was quite decided: 'none of these palaces are as livable as Babelsberg'.[28]

Standing in the most famous room, the grotto, one is inclined to agree with her. It invites a party but is certainly not cosy or snug. When it is lit up the light

ABOVE: The most famous room in the Neues
Palais, the grotto, encrusted with semiprecious
stones and writhing sea monsters whose scales
are made up of thousands of shells. Even the
doors glitter with false stalactites.

LEFT: 'Queen Victoria often suffered
from "racking headaches" on her travels.
I think this was certainly the only time I wished
her captivating spell were slightly less
powerful. It was, however, soothing to sit
in this cool, cavernous grotto.'

glances off the cascading patterns of shells on the walls, and the semiprecious stones in the rustications glitter darkly. The roof echoes, the candelabra swirl. Cool waters seem to flow across the floor: merely an optical illusion created by the sinuous patterns in the multi-coloured marble. The chill strikes up through shoes; homely it is not. The mists gather outside in the park, along the formal rides and between the trees where half-cleaned sculptures appear white in the gloom, and the streetlights of the town are only the size of candle flames in the far distance.

We tread through dim, deserted rooms, their gilding rubbed back to the reddish bole underneath, their shabby paintwork cracked and peeling but growing old gracefully. 'There is a theatre in the palace', said Queen Victoria, 'and many splendid Fêtes have been given here for the Emperor and Empress of Russia, even till last year, which helped to bring on the King's last serious illness.'[29] It is warm in the theatre, and the lights don't work. Tired after our long day, we sit down on the front row of comfortable, thick, red velvet seats stamped with the Prussian eagle. In the gloom on stage we can just make out the half-rolled-up set of the *Marriage of Figaro*. It is calm and peaceful and we rest there for a while, sensing a silent audience around us.

Driving towards Berlin, our sense of sadness that the beautiful buildings of Potsdam have been left quietly to rot alters; it was nice to see cobblestones and so much that has not changed for fifty years and more unspoilt by the West, with its neon signs, and still giving a feeling of the past.

We go back across the Glienicke Bridge, where East and West used to glare at one another across the ideological gulf. It is still a forbidding place, with marching imperialist columns and the heavy arches of the iron bridge which has replaced the one Queen Victoria painted from her sitting room window. Something of the old atmosphere of fear and suspicion haunts the place, and it seems somehow symbolic of the confusions of history and ideology that here, once, you could go eastwards and enter (though with difficulty) an ideological West.

Just across the bridge is Klein Glienicke, built in the 1820s by Prince Charles, brother of the Crown Prince, to house his collection of antique Greek sculpture. Victoria and Albert drove one morning to breakfast here at the casino by the lakeside with Fritz's wicked uncle, whose innuendoes and jokes made even married princesses blush, and who wasn't safe to be entrusted with the care of the Prince of Wales on a shooting expedition ('imagine what company, what a tone and what conversation').[30] The view from the casino is quite unchanged. We are now in what was the old West German sector, and

'A most lovely evening, after a very hot day, and the same sharp clearness in the air, which was so striking at Paris, and which we have not got in England.'

21 AUGUST 1858

The terrace at Glienicke. (Watercolour by C. Graeb.) This view is quite unchanged today, and it is easy to imagine the Queen breakfasting in this 'charming spot, just outside the Casino, close above the water, with a beautiful view. Excellent coffee, cakes and fancy bread, as at Babelsberg, and in most places in Germany.' (Journal, 21 August 1858.)

the difference in the upkeep of the palatial relics of the Ancien Régime is striking: fresh paint, gilded knobs on the fences, manicured lawns. Even the unkempt areas give the impression that they have been left like that deliberately, because it is ecologically sound rather than because money or manpower is lacking.

Victoria did not return to Berlin for thirty years, until 1888. Since 1871 the crown prince had been Emperor William I; he was now dead and Fritz had succeeded him. The Queen stayed at Charlottenburg, in rooms which Vicky had furnished for her in the apartments of Frederick the Great (truly his ghost haunts every royal building in this city), and which had hot been used since his day. The palace was bombed in 1943 and fighting took place in the gardens during the battle of Berlin. Charlottenburg has since been painstakingly restored down to the last carved and gilded flower petal, using old plans and drawings, and the figure of Victory once more stands triumphantly on the very top.

Queen Victoria again drove through the Brandenburg Gate, which had

This watercolour, above right, by Michael Max shows Charlottenburg, in Berlin, of which the Queen wrote, 'though the situation is not pretty, it is to my taste far the most cheerful of the Palaces'. (Journal, 20 August 1858.) It was badly damaged in the Second World War, and subsequently completely rebuilt.

made a strong impression on her so many years earlier. Today its imposing silhouette has become a potent symbol of the destruction of the wall that divided the city. On the far side, in the old eastern sector, there is a street market selling off Red Army souvenirs, the flotsam and jetsam of the ebbing tide of empire.

When she first drove up Unter den Linden, the street which leads from the Brandenburg Gate to what was the heart of royal Berlin, Queen Victoria had called it 'the Bond Street of Berlin, a broad street with trees . . . very fine and gay, with pretty shops'.[31] Thirty years later she remembered it 'so well', driving along it on her way to see Vicky's palace. This she had inspected in 1858 in its half-finished state and had pronounced it 'very comfortably arranged, and on the English principle – thanks to us'.[32] By 1888 her standards seem to have risen: 'The house, as well as the hall, are fine, but there are no really large or good rooms in it. They are beautifully furnished and full of works of art.'[33]

Queen Victoria's second visit to Berlin was a very gloomy one. It was here that she heard of the death of her courier, Kanné, and she had come because she knew that Fritz was dying. Queen Victoria paid a visit to his widowed mother in the Berlin schloss: 'I went up in a lift, alone, and there was the Empress, in deep mourning, with a long veil, seated in a chair, quite crumpled up and deathly pale, really rather a ghastly sight.'[34] Vicky and Fritz had begun their married life at the schloss (with Queen Victoria fussing long-distance about fresh air and hot stoves and German christening customs and a liberal Germany) while their own house was made ready. The building was obliterated during the Second World War and now all that is found on the site are the fun fair and the wheel of fortune.

Arrival of Queen Victoria at Charlottenburg, 1888, to visit her dying son-in-law, the Emperor Frederick. With her are her daughters, Princess Beatrice and Empress Frederick (Vicky), and her eldest grandson, William, who would so soon succeed his father.

CHAPTER SIX

The Late Holidays, 1861—1899

Rendezvous at Darmstadt

In 1860, after a visit to Coburg, Queen Victoria considered buying an estate there to make Albert's birthplace a sort of rendezvous for the family. But after his death in December the following year she did not have the heart to do anything more than return to Coburg in search of some reflection of her lost happiness: 'Such precious recollections crowded in on me. Everything seems to breathe and speak of my beloved one, in this his *own* old home, which I quite feel as if it were mine too!'[1]

It was instead Darmstadt which really became the rendezvous for it was there that her second daughter, Princess Alice, had gone to live in 1861 after her marriage to Prince Louis of Hesse, and it was much more conveniently situated than Coburg. The Queen could conduct her matriarchal business en route to or from her holidays elsewhere, and would often spend no more than the day in Darmstadt, go to the station at about seven or eight o'clock in the evening, and continue overnight on the train.

We leave Coburg on a crisp, sunny morning, and head for Darmstadt. On the way, to remind us what to expect, we read the entry in Queen Victoria's journal in which she describes her first visit to Alice in Darmstadt, on her way home from Coburg in 1863:

Stopped at a station just outside the splendid park . . . or rather more woods, full of splendid trees, reminding one of parts of the Windsor and Richmond parks, and again of some of the French forests, to the Jagd Schloss [hunting lodge] of Kranichstein. It is a curious old house with gable ends, built round three sides of a court, with a pond near it. It is very comfortable inside and has many long corridors, full of magnificent stags' horns. How these would have interested Albert, as well as the curious old

Darmstadt, *c*.1890.
FROM LEFT: Prince
Henry of Battenberg,
Princess Beatrice,
Princess Alix of Hesse,
a coachman, Francis
Clark, Ernst Ludwig
Hereditary Grand Duke
of Hesse, Queen Victoria,
Victoria Princess Louis
of Battenberg, Grand
Duke of Hesse, an
Indian attendant.

family pictures! We breakfasted in a curious room in a turret, a few steps up out of the drawing room.[2]

How rural and peaceful this sounds; another visitor described it as 'a simple little place, and so thoroughly in the forest that wild boars sometimes drank from the water under the windows'.[3]

But Darmstadt is not like Coburg. It is one of the satellites of Frankfurt, its motorways slicing through what is left of the flat countryside. The suburbs have crept out to the edge of the woods, which is more a green belt than an enchanted forest where stags might glimmer in the distance and savage boar rustle in the undergrowth.

The hunting lodge, charming and intimate, about the size of a large farmstead ennobled with a curly gable, is part museum (devoted to the history

The White Room in the old schloss in Darmstadt. (Watercolour by Franz Huth, 1917.) Once its splendours were similar to those at Ehrenburg, but sadly it was destroyed in World War II.

of hunting) and part hotel. At the little station of Darmstadt-Kranichstein Queen Victoria's special train would puff and screech to a halt, and stand there steaming as she descended stiffly onto the platform in her black dress and bonnet. It is now a run-down collection of buildings housing a railway museum, which at certain times has 'operation days', when its steam locomotives are taken out and once again you hear the sounds which would have been so familiar to her.

In later years the Queen did sometimes stay at Darmstadt for longer than a

few hours, as in 1880, when she came for the confirmation of Alice's two eldest daughters, the princesses Victoria and Elizabeth of Hesse. She stayed in the old schloss in the centre of Darmstadt, and left a description of it in her journal: 'One drives into a narrow court, and up onto the ramparts, to a small private door, where a short flight of steps takes one into a Drawing Room.' The place was crowded with relations, for Her Majesty's presence at the rites of passage of the reigning family of this small dukedom would draw royalty from all over Europe.

Although her sitting room, bedroom and dressing room, all conveniently en suite, were 'nice rooms' and everything had been done to make them comfortable, she did not approve of their outlook onto a closed courtyard through which the public had a right to walk, as was customary in many ducal palaces in Germany. The glockenspiel clock in the courtyard, which played tunes every half hour, was stopped during the night for her benefit. The corridor which ran along outside her room was 'interminable', and hung with old family portraits. Everyone was busy getting ready for the confirmation service and the Queen observed that 'there was the same excitement and bustle as at home, when we have any state function, only less punctuality, and more long waiting'.[4]

Their confirmation was an important event in the princesses' lives, but not necessarily one that their grandmother would have attended had their mother still been alive. It was a very sad story. In 1878 two of Alice's children, Ernst Ludwig and May, had caught diphtheria; she had worn herself out nursing them, and then the four-year-old May had died. Alice had tried to keep the news from Ernst Ludwig, but he had asked so often how his sister was that she had been forced to tell him; in comforting him, in spite of all cautioning, she had kissed him and so caught the infection herself. He lived, she died – by hideous coincidence on 14 December, the anniversary of the day of Albert's death. Now the Queen felt that she must take a special interest in these motherless grandchildren, of whom there were five left, Victoria, Elizabeth (or 'Ella'), Irène, Ernst Ludwig and Alix.

Having seen Victoria and Ella make their Christian vows, Queen Victoria went to pay her sorrowful respects at her daughter's mausoleum at the Rosenhohe, the Hill of Roses, a tranquil resting place today, guarded by a row of spectacular Jugendstil lions. The mausoleums of the Dukes of Hesse-Darmstadt are grouped in a garden here, and Alice lies in a modest neoclassical building, not really to Queen Victoria's taste, nor dignified enough: 'very small', she called it, 'in a bare, plain Grecian style'. She brought a cross of violets and a wreath of immortelles, and knelt in front of the crimson velvet pall that covered her daughter's coffin: 'I felt terribly shaken. It seemed too dreadful!'[5]

And there was 'darling Alice's palace' to visit as well, where everything was 'so tastefully done, and planned out by darling Alice herself', whose rooms were now almost as much of a mausoleum as Rosenhohe. The Queen went up to her daughter's 'lovely sitting room, where we had sat together so happily, four years ago! All the things on her table, letters etc., all left, and *she* gone! Then went to her bedroom, where all has been placed again, as it was. It was quite overwhelming.'[6]

She saw reminders of Alice everywhere: 'This new part of the town, reminds me of England, and was dear Alice's work. She planned and encouraged all the improvements, and the houses are very pretty. Everywhere, traces of her mind are to be noticed! Like her dear father!'[7]

On one occasion when there was not enough room for her in 'darling Alice's palace', she stayed not in the schloss but the Alte Palais, 'which is rather dull and gloomy in comparison with the Neues Palais'; the furniture was 'stiff and old-fashioned' and it was 'rather noisy being close to the Luisenplatz'.[8]

We sweep through the centre of Darmstadt on wide roads; it has a bleak, characterless look. The high red and white walls of the schloss come into view, looking much as we expect from the journal. We recognize the courtyard, the ramparts and the private entrance (this last a little grassy from lack of use, certainly, but still here); the glockenspiel sounds its carillon from the tower, every four hours either a chorale or a folksong. And yet, all is not as it seems. The old schloss, a typical palatial agglomeration of neoclassical additions to a renaissance core, which the last grand duke turned into a museum in 1924, went the same way as much of the rest of the centre of Darmstadt in the firestorm of 1944. Most of the schloss was painstakingly rebuilt and the museum was re-opened in 1964. Where the state rooms used to be there is now a library and archives, and the White Room, reminiscent of the throne room in Coburg, where the Queen received the King of Prussia in 1865, has shrunk to a postcard of a watercolour painting on the ticket collector's desk. Among the treasures and curios on display in the museum are five really extraordinary survivals of holocaust and mayhem, the bearded sporrans belonging to the Grand Duke Louis which he wore when he came to stay with his mother-in-law at Balmoral.

You feel that you are never far away from the effects of the wartime bombs in the centre of Darmstadt, particularly when you are tracing lost palaces in the town with the aid of a guide book for 1886. In the pedestrian precincts in the centre are curious circles about twenty feet across, marked out by the pattern of the paving bricks, and in some places vast, circular, twisted forms can be seen embedded in the pavement, a reminder that on 11 September 1944 Darmstadt was hit by thousands of incendiary bombs and hundreds of high-explosive bombs.

Another casualty of the firestorm was the Neues Palais, where Queen Victoria stayed in 1884 for the wedding of Princess Victoria to Louis, Prince of Battenberg. She felt 'quite at home' at the 'dear, comfortable Neues Palais':[9] 'I have got, as sitting room, darling Alice's lovely one, left just as she had it, with all her things still lying about, which I recognized, and I am writing, lying on her own comfortable sofa. The sitting room opens into her bedroom, the sacred room, where she left this world. My charming bedroom, was once, one of the nurseries.'[10] The Queen seems to speak from a vanished world, and yet she is not so very far away, for when she returned in 1885 it was not only for the confirmation of Ernst Ludwig (who would one day become that last grand duke) but also for the christening of the first baby from the previous year's marriage. This baby was Alice, who would one day be the mother of the present Duke of Edinburgh. The links between Darmstadt and Windsor are still close, and every May the German cousins visit their English relations.

Wherever the Queen stayed her daily routine continued as normal, and she would drive out for carriage exercise just as she did at home. Only fragments of the Darmstadt that she knew remain, like the Orangerie (every prince had to cultivate the golden apples of the Hesperides, and show that he was rich enough to heat whole houses for them during cold, northern winters) and Prince Emil's garden, where Queen Victoria heard nightingales among the lilacs.

One day she called in to the Roman Catholic church (which dates from 1827) to see 'the fine marble monument with a recumbent statue of the late Grand Duchess Mathilde'. As forthright as ever, she called it 'an ugly circular church, a copy of the Pantheon . . . the interior is as ugly as the exterior'.[11] This too went the way of so much else, all but its outer walls completely destroyed by the bomb attack on 11 September 1944. It has since been rebuilt, but the restoration here has not attempted slavishly to replicate the original; the expense would have been far too great and, besides, the way it has been done tells its story. The wooden dome was replaced with one in the material of the 1950s, reinforced concrete, and on one section of the interior, like a patch on a garment, a replica of the original coffered construction has been inserted. The top of the dome is glassed and looks as fragile as a new baby's cranium, and hovering in this clear space is a vast, angular dove.

The Rebirth of Schloss Braunshardt

So much having been obliterated, we follow Queen Victoria on another of her afternoon drives without much optimism. Braunshardt, she explained in her journal, was:

> one of the many houses belonging to Louis built in the last century, and has curious small rococo rooms, of different colours, with family pictures. Here we took tea, which we had brought with us. Went into the grounds, where there is a curious open air theatre, and the lawn is composed of steps cut in the ground for the audience to sit on, and surrounded by hedges. In olden times theatrical performances were given there. There was also a sort of 'Merry go round' and Giant's [?] stride.[12]

Alice's husband, Louis IV, had inherited the house and the title of Grand Duke of Hesse-Darmstadt from his eccentric uncle, Louis III, who had bought Braunshardt in 1865, even though he had numerous other country houses and

'The rococo rooms of Schloss Braunshardt, which the Queen regarded with such curiosity, have been re-awakened like Sleeping Beauty and restored in loving detail. In this room are the fragile window panes, which have miraculously survived the ravages of time and war, where three young princesses, full of mischievous gaiety, scratched their names in the glass.'

The same room in 1872, when the old Grand Duke of Hesse, though he lived in Darmstadt, kept each of his numerous country houses ready for occupation, visiting each in turn. (Watercolour by Heinrich Kröh.)

hunting lodges. He lived in the schloss in Darmstadt and would visit in turn each of his other residences. Even if he only went for the day he would take with him – besides food and cooks in a baggage waggon – his valet, his hairdresser and the man who looked after his pipes.[13] So you could say that in bringing their tea with them, Queen Victoria and her party were doing no more than was traditional.

Braunshardt lies a couple of miles out of Darmstadt. Flat fields with no hedges surround the small village, whose old nucleus has been swallowed up by new, not particularly attractive, building. We drive round and round what appears to be a housing estate. Enthusiasm wanes. We draw up outside a high wall, and press the largest of the rank of doorbells below the intercom. Blank walls, houses crowding in along a village street – we will find nothing here.

How wrong we are; for when we step inside Schloss Braunshardt we enter those very same 'curious small rococo rooms, of different colours', a rainbow interior: a blue room, a violet room, an apricot and rose room, a green salon and a garden room of clambering, trellised flowers, touched here and there

RIGHT: Princess Alix of Hesse, March 1880, granddaughter of Queen Victoria and one day to become the last Tsarina of Russia. (Photograph by Backofen.) ABOVE: She was the youngest of three princesses who left their childhood signature in the watery old glass of Braunshardt.

with silver and gold. We look out through watery panes of glass which distort and make mysterious the broad daylight outside. Scratched in one of the panes, such frail survivors of time and war, are three spidery names; 'Victoria', 'Irène' and 'Alix' : three mischievous young princesses, one wet afternoon, perhaps, inscribing their signatures with a diamond on the glass which might even then have been more than a hundred years old. 'Alix', the youngest, would grow up into the melancholy, intense beauty who captured the heart of the Tsarevitch, became the last Tsarina of Russia and, with her husband and children, would come to a violent end at Ekaterinburg in 1917.

There are toys scattered on the floor of the primrose yellow room, and conkers from the chestnut trees in the garden. The best thing about this house is that it is alive. It is not a museum; it is a home. But there is no time to stop and ponder for we are greeted by a whirlwind, Freiherr von Maltzahn, who lives here with his wife and two daughters, and who has brought Braunshardt to its present condition.

He has the bright gleam of the fanatic in his blue eyes, and he fairly crackles with energy. He sets off like a firework, exploding with enthusiasm and love for his house, his Sleeping Beauty, as he calls it, and takes us on a spontaneous tour of the work that he has done. We are given a first-hand account of what is required in terms of devotion, energy and money to restore a building. Turning back the clock, digging out and recreating the past, is not a business for the fainthearted.

When he bought Braunshardt from the Roman Catholic Church in 1986 he became its twelfth owner. The house, built between 1760 and 1763, had had a chequered history; it had belonged intermittently to the grand dukes, had passed into the hands of a university professor and subsquently had housed at different times delinquent girls, possibly the Gestapo, war refugees, old age pensioners and religious students. By then it was in a sorry state, with woodworm, rotten timbers and sagging ceilings, and nobody wanted it. Except for the man with the gleam in his eye. There were sixty holes in the roof and the water was pouring in, threatening the precious rococo moulded plaster ceilings underneath. Previous occupants had left their mark: the professor had put in a false ceiling, the Church had built forty little cells for private study and devotion, and other occupants had vandalized it in various ways.

As Freiherr von Maltzahn gives you some appalling statistic concerning the repairs – how many hundreds of loads of rubble he and his helpers took out, or how many hundreds of thousands of deutschmarks each room cost – his hands fly up in the air and he explodes with laughter, doubling up at the joke. His blue eyes sparkle and he produces armfuls of books and folders relating to the restoration work, together with a detailed survey of the house that fills five fat files. He hastens to describe the excitement of unbricking doorways and finding the original doors still there, handles and locks complete. His eyes dance as he describes how they steamed off the layers of paint and dirt that clogged up the delicate plaster ceilings, all of which were cleaned with dental equipment. The plasterwork was then repainted and regilded with the colours found underneath, each room taking six months to complete.

As has happened at Brühl, he has put the clock back to the date when the house was built, when its most romantic occupant, the future Queen Louise of Prussia, lived here and watched from an upstairs window the battle of Mainz, in which her fiancé was engaged in fighting the onslaught of Napoleon.

The soft colours of the rooms at Braunshardt speak of another age, and yet it is a house that is lived in and loved as a home. As can be seen from the dust-cover, the finishing touches have still to be made.

Work is still in progress, and there is still much to do. The bones of part of the baroque garden remain – the chestnut trees that provided the conkers, for instance – though the green theatre described by Queen Victoria has long since vanished. The ceiling of the green salon sags dangerously and the sunken marble bath beyond the garden room is dry and choked with debris. The Sleeping Beauty is not yet fully awake; Germans refer to this fairy story as the legend of the Thorny Rose, which, considering the trouble anyone faces in restoring an ancient building, is perhaps a better term. But Freiherr von Maltzahn is the man for the job, for a man who can persuade you to stand in a pit filled with rubble and see the exotic luxury of an eighteenth-century sunken marble bath is a man with a talent.

He estimates that at the end of his project, his Thorny Rose will have cost him over six million marks, or around two and a half million pounds. 'But then', he says, 'you will have something which is prepared for the next hundred years'. 'And a beautiful place to live', we add. 'Yes', he says, 'every morning we get up, we just pinch each other!' Then he grows serious, 'You start to live with it: you are internally proud about this, and happy, but it is an obligation, a kind of inheritance to keep and to bring it to the next generation. It will, we hope, belong to our children, and we hope, be in hands where it will be kept in the right way, lived in and loved, in the right way.'

In Search of Queen Victoria's Lime Tree

Not long after she visited Braunshardt Queen Victoria made another, rather longer, excursion from Darmstadt. Today the journey takes only twenty minutes. On the way we pass the range of low, wooded hills which hide the Schloss Heiligenberg, a summer retreat that looks like a little white Osborne beside a crescent-shaped lake, a cool and leafy place. Queen Victoria once came here to visit her granddaughter Victoria and her handsome husband Louis. It is now a beautifully kept teacher-training college.

We turn off the road at the village of Bensheim and wind up a small wooded valley. This is really the most unlikely episode in all our searches. We are looking for a tree, which we hope to find in the grounds of Schloss Schönberg, but first we have to find the schloss. It has sunk into obscurity, and all we have to guide us is a rather hesitant watercolour (it is noticeable how the quality of commissions changes after the death of Albert) and some vague directions.

We drive along the valley peering upwards in the hope of seeing turrets among the treetops. A glimpse of a witch's-hat roof and a stepped gable suggests we might be on the right track, but when we eventually stop we are in an unprepossessing cul-de-sac and the road has dwindled to a footpath. We walk the last bit, asking ourselves if this can really be right. Just as we are sure we are on a wild goose chase we round the last corner, and there it is: 'a regular old burg and one drives in under an archway, on to a sort of terrace, which goes the whole length of the house, and is planted with flowers and shrubs'.[14] The schloss still answers Queen Victoria's accurate description today. There is no one about.

Carved in grey stone over the door by which the Queen entered is the date 1540. Inside, 'the winding corkscrew staircase' reminded her of the Rosenau. 'The house is very old,' she wrote, 'the most ancient part dating from the twelfth and thirteenth centuries and the latest being two hundred years old ... Most of the rooms are small and low, but very comfortably and nicely arranged. There are many family pictures in the house.'[15]

In visiting Schönberg Queen Victoria was tracing her links with what had seemed to us an obscure branch in her family tree: 'here', she wrote, 'my great Grandmother, Princess Caroline of Erbach, who married Prince Reuss Ebersdorf, was born. She was the mother of my dear Grandmama of Coburg-Saalfeld.' We get a bit lost in this pedigree thicket until we remember that we have seen the portrait of 'My dear Grandmama of Coburg-Saalfeld' in the Family Hall in the Ehrenburg; hers was the capable, clever face looking out of

Schönberg, outside
Bensheim, where Queen
Victoria's great-
grandmother was born.
The Queen called it 'a
regular old burg' and was
reminded of the Rosenau
as she climbed the
corkscrew stair.
(Watercolour by
H. Schlegel.)

the portrait next to the one of Albert. It was she who had nine children, took her daughters to Russia and virtually ran the duchy of Coburg. The roots of Queen Victoria's family trees, and those of her descendants, are entwined and interwoven very tight.

She continues: 'We went out to look at the beautiful view from the terrace, and walked in the gardens, where I planted a tree.' The view from the terrace is nothing much today, the valley is overgrown. The place is currently being converted from a sanatorium for miners into a school. Over quaint and curious doorways, up and down little stairways and through cobbled passageways are busy little signs saying Entry, Exit or Kitchen. The shrubs on the terrace are clipped, and the lawns are neat but there is no answer from behind the caretaker's lace curtains. An air of melancholy hangs over it all; the castle seems withdrawn and a little forlorn.

The gardens, part formal, part English landscape style, are close by, and not far into them we come across a tall, flourishing lime tree. Translated, the plaque on it reads 'Victoria Lime: This lime tree was planted by Her Majesty Queen Victoria of England on the occasion of her visit to the Schloss 1887 to honour her great-grandfather Count George Auguste of Erbach-Schönberg, the founder of this park.' It is not quite accurate: she made her visit in 1885, and the count (1691–1758) was her great-great-grandfather.

'It was rather wonderful to see this thriving lime tree which Queen Victoria planted, and to think that perhaps one day the trees I have planted will be as tall and beautiful.'

The Villa Clara at Baveno

Besides Braunshardt, there was only one place that we visited which is still in private hands and still a home, and that was in another country.

After Alice's death, the Queen decided that she needed a complete change of scenery. She was nearly sixty, and she had never seen Italy. The Italian lakes had long been famous for their beauty and climate, and she accepted the offer of a villa just outside the modest resort of Baveno, on the shores of Lake Maggiore.

It is very late by the time we arrive there; the journey from Milan seems to have lasted an age. For the final few miles the road runs along the side of Lake Maggiore, and over on the other shore the mountains are darkly visible, their lower slopes strung with lights which shine down into the black, silky water. We stay at the Grand Hotel Dino, built on the site of the Hotel Bellevue, which the Queen mentions, 'close upon the lake'.[16] The next morning we can see even less of the far-famed beauties of Maggiore and the fabled Borromean Islands: fog encloses us.

Just outside Baveno ('the merest village', the Queen called it[17]) we turn off the main road and zigzag up between large evergreens, slightly shaggy lawns and mossy garden statuary. We are not travelling in the same season as Queen Victoria did; she came in the spring, when the gardens were ablaze with azaleas and camellias, but the mists and gentle melancholy of autumn make our nostalgic travels all the more atmospheric.

We round the last dripping shrub, and the Villa Clara (to use the name that it had in Queen Victoria's day) lies before us. It cannot quite make up its mind which architectural style to adopt, and is perhaps best described as European. Its bright red brick, honey-coloured stone window casings and grey slates are all very English but the arcaded entrance porch and loggia are Renaissance Italian, the dormer windows with the lacy ironwork along the top of the mansard roofs are French and the dotty pinnacle is familiar German. The general effect is of St Pancras on holiday. Local opinion, however, proudly declares that it is Scottish.

Two huge black Newfoundland dogs lumber out, friendly and curious. A maple tree blazes like an autumn bonfire beside the porch to which Queen Victoria and her party drove up on 28

The Villa Clara, Baveno, March 1879, lent to the Queen by Charles Henfrey. (Watercolour by Gabriel Carelli.)

March 1879. She was welcomed on the steps by the owner. 'Mr Henfrey', she wrote, 'is a very quiet and unassuming oldish gentleman. I thanked him for his kindness, in lending me his charming house, and he said "it is a great honour for me, I wish it were more worthy".'[18]

Charles Henfrey, born the year before the Queen, had made his money building railways in India and Italy. He had built the Villa Clara and called it after his wife. Having given the Queen the freedom of his house he would have stayed elsewhere while she was in residence.

The terrace of the Villa Clara, with the view of the Sasso del Ferro and the Isola dei Pescatori. (Watercolour by Gabriel Carelli.) 'The rooms open out on a loggia', wrote the Queen, 'both above and below, which is painted quite in the Italian style. It is quite fairy-like, sitting and gazing out on to the lovely scenery.'

'The nice Swiss housekeeper', the Queen continued, 'showed us to our rooms. There is a long corridor, at the end of which are my bedroom, dressing room and boudoir, en suite. Beatrice and the ladies are opposite, and the gentlemen upstairs. The view from the windows is magnificent. The Lake stretches out before one, the splendid high mountans, rising up behind, tipped with snow.'[19]

Villa Clara, elegant and secluded, was perfect for her: 'this is really a charming house', she said;[20]

the rooms have painted ceilings and cornices . . . The furniture is simple and handsome, of light carved wood. The Drawing Room, has bow windows, is very prettily furnished and arranged. All the floors are of mosaic, over which carpets are laid. There are fine old pictures in the corridors, and some lovely watercolours in the rooms upstairs. Mine, is a small narrow boudoir, with cabinets full of pretty things. The rooms open out on a loggia, both above and below, which is painted quite in the Italian style. It is quite fairy-like, sitting and gazing out on to the lovely scenery.[21]

'Close to the cool waters of this pool at the Villa Clara we found the exquisite little church, built out of the pink and white granite for which Baveno is famous, where Queen Victoria would attend service on Sundays. It was quiet and peaceful there, a place to be alone and give thanks for the gifts that life brings.'

We in our turn are made welcome by the current owners, the Conte Branca and his charming wife. The villa has been in their family for a hundred years. The furniture is still handsome and simple, and the house is very much lived in – the family papers piled on tables, games and tennis rackets propped up in corners under the painted cornices, and the huge dogs slither in over the polished mosaic, to be sent out again with all the emphasis that only Italians can master.

The mists are clearing; it is a joy to see again. Through the magnificent trees we get glimpses of water, but we do not have the unobstructed view that we expected. Knowing the place through paintings done more than a century ago, it is disconcerting to find that saplings have suddenly mushroomed into forest giants. They, like the villa, have preservation orders on them, and cannot be touched without the permission of the Italian authorities.

And what of the 'pretty little church, a private one, built, and belonging to, Mr Henfrey'?[22] We walk up the garden, the two huge dogs joined by 'Speedy', a bossy little brown one, and there it is, just the same, built in the Byzantine style using the pink and white granite for which Baveno is famous. The

Baveno and the Isola dei Pescatori. (Watercolour by V. Ripari.) For the first time Queen Victoria was in Italy, and her 'bright dream' of many years had at last been realized.

interior, which is richly decorated, with white angels flying in gold mosaic over the altar, is lit up by the sunshine that now beams in through stained-glass windows. We try the organ – made by Messrs Bishop and Starr, by Appointment to HRH the Princess of Wales (later Queen Alexandra) – but the notes come out cracked and wheezy. This is really a place to be quiet and peaceful, and enjoy the beauty around us.

The mists have cleared and we can see the famous views at last. The calm surface of the lake ripples gently; each mountain is wearing a plume of cloud like knights going in to joust, and halfway across the water float the hazy woods and spires of the Borromean Islands. So often it is all hidden by fog or rain, and poor Queen Victoria suffered just like everyone else: 'three wet days running and such rain as I never saw anywhere else – torrents without ceasing'.[23] But when the weather cleared she could write to her daughter Vicky: 'On Thursday we went in a steamer up to the very end of the lake into Switzerland where the Swiss Alps rise beautifully in their eternal snow. I recognized those I had seen from the other side in '68! We went as far as Locarno. Anything like the views and colours here I never saw. They really are quite marvellous.'[24]

Stone cutters, Luna Marina. (Watercolour by Gabriel Carelli.) The granite, which the Queen saw being worked beside the lake, is still being quarried from the mountains behind Baveno.

Her constant companion was, as ever, Princess Beatrice, on whom she relied for support and company. Even a day's absence mattered: 'Beatrice', wrote the Queen, 'without whom I felt very dull, returned, delighted with her expedition.'[25] One wonders if Beatrice, only twenty-two, felt the pressure of being relied on so much. The Queen was very concerned at this time for Vicky, who had just lost a son: 'My poor dear darling child, my heart bleeds and aches for you to that extent I cannot describe it.'[26]

Queen Victoria could not escape the pressures of family life, nor entirely disengage herself from the demands of her position. She went to Monza to greet the King and Queen of Italy, who had come all the way from Rome to see her; it was the first time since Albert's death, she wrote, 'that I had been to anything of the kind. I felt dreadfully nervous.'[27] The mother of the Queen of Italy, the Duchess of Genoa, paid Queen Victoria a formal call at the villa in immensely grand style – postilions in blue velvet, four splendid black horses, footmen in long scarlet cloaks. She was entertained in the drawing room and the visit lasted for half an hour. The Queen was really much happier in the garden among the azaleas, where lizards darted about in the sun. She tried out her rusty Italian: 'Talked to the undergardener and was proud at getting on so

*'The rugged, very high
peaked Alps, crowned
by the Simplon, covered
with snow, rise up in
grand towering masses
before one.'*

29 MARCH 1879

The Queen's journal recounts how one
afternoon her carriage 'turned up a rough
road, close by the river Toce. Here we
stopped for nearly an hour, while I sketched
the glorious view towards the Simplon'. She
inscribed her painting, 'Near to the Toce
looking towards the Simplon', and dated it 5
April 1879.

Mergozzo, 1992. On 9 April 1879 Queen
Victoria admired 'The pretty small Lago di
Mergozzo, which was quite a picture,
reminding me much, of our dear Highland
Lochs, only that at the head of it is a quaint
little village town with its piazza and
campanile, the high and still snow-tipped
peaks of the Alps, rising up behind'.

well with my Italian. Was able to ask questions about all the plants and trees, and understood him perfectly.'[28]

'Sketching and painting, trying to catch the effect of the ever changing lights, on the lovely scenery.'

9 APRIL 1879

At home she could be as private and simple as she liked; in public she could not. Her sightseeing trip to Milan was a complete failure. After a 'tedious long drive of an hour and a quarter' to the station at Arona she endured a 'monotonous' train journey to Milan in the rain, managed to see Leonardo's *Last Supper*, 'sadly faded and injured, still … greatly to be admired', was 'positively mobbed' in Milan Cathedral and had 'regularly to hurry down to the Crypt' where the crowd could be kept out. Here she was treated to a view of the shrivelled flesh and gorgeous vestments of San Carlo Borromeo, 'rather a ghastly spectacle, though there is nothing disagreeable or repulsive'.[29]

Afterwards her private secretary, Sir Henry Ponsonby, received a thundering note of displeasure, at 'that dreadful crowding in the Cathedral', Her Majesty expressing pungently and illegibly her wishes to be private.[30] The difficulty was, as he pointed out, though not to her, that 'if she had gone as Queen we might have had fifty police there, but she had repeated over and over that she would go quite privately – so there were only a few police – enough to keep them back, but not enough to prevent them crowding round'.[31]

The people of Baveno, because it was a small place, were more polite. When she went out walking with Beatrice 'the people never bother or follow one'.[32] She would walk through the village to 'a place where the granite is worked, close to the Lake. The masons sit under large tile roofed sheds, making beautiful pillars.'[33]

The granite is everywhere in Baveno; even the steps under our feet are made of it. We are standing in the sun under the window which was once Queen Victoria's bedroom, reading our notes from her journal, with little lizards running in and out of the cracks in the stone. We read about her drives in the neighbouring countryside, to various 'picturesque' villages. 'The children on the roads know me quite well, and call out "La Regina d'Inghilterra". There are such dreadful queer looking pigs here, with quite long legs. Two mounted Carabinieri generally follow the carriage at some little distance, and ones on foot patrol the roads. They look very smart and well turned out.'[34]

Her excursions were not all they might have been. As always, on the box of her carriage, in tam-o'-shanter and kilt – full Highland fig – sat John Brown, who loathed being abroad. At one lovely spot she did not get out of the carriage, it was supposed by Sir Henry, 'because Brown would not allow her to get out. He is surly beyond measure and today we could see him all the way – a beautiful drive – with his eyes fixed on the horses' tails refusing to look up.'[35]

It was not always so; one evening they stopped, wrote the Queen, for 'nearly an hour, while I sketched the glorious view towards the Simplon'.[36] The combination of lake and mountain always sent her hurrying for her paintbox; here, she felt, one could sketch 'all day and never be satisfied with the

Over the years the Queen had not lost her interest in people. On 20 April 1879 she wrote in her journal, 'sketched in the colonade, a pretty girl of 15, called Teresa Morandi . . . she talked a good deal of her mother who had had 12 children, but lost a great number of them. She came from Roncarno and said she had already been drawn by "due Donne Inglesi".'

result'.[37] It must have been very peaceful sitting here painting on the terrace. She also sketched a local beauty, Teresa Morandi, and gave her a shawl to thank her for modelling.

We eat a delicious, very Italian lunch – pasta and artichoke hearts, fish from the lake and sweet chestnuts – with the Branca family and their friends, and it is time to leave the Villa Clara.

On the way to our next destination we pass the dramatic and colossal statue of San Carlo Borromeo at Arona, which the Queen herself had seen on her way to the villa.

The Côte d'Azur

Queen Victoria enjoyed her southern holidays, and as the years went by they became an annual event. In 1882, three years after her visit to the Villa Clara, she went to the south of France for the first time, and for the first time set eyes on the Mediterranean. She tried various resorts – Menton, Hyères, Cannes, Grasse – all along what came to be known as the Côte d'Azur, coming to rest in her very old age on the heights of Cimiez, above Nice.

It is late at night as we drive on to the south of France, the last part along the Corniche, the road engineered by Napoleon to march his armies through a region so rugged and inaccessible that Dante had once used it as a metaphor for purgatory.

But it is more like heaven to wake the next morning and sit outside with the sun streaming down through the umbrella pines which roof the terrace, and on the table a hot golden croissant offering temptation. Exhaustion and stress seem to melt away in the sun.

In Queen Victoria's day the south of France was indeed visited for its health-giving properties, and people usually came here in the winter, on the advice of their doctor, to escape the rigours of northern climates. One of the first established health resorts was Menton (then part of Italy and known as Mentone), close to the Italian border, where the climate was especially mild and balmy. This is where Queen Victoria came in 1882. Once again, she stayed in a house belonging to Mr Henfrey, the Chalet des Rosiers. Let her take up the story of her arrival:

> Leaving Marseilles one enters a mountain range, which is very fine, and the line runs through beautiful country. Most striking it was, when one came suddenly upon the sea, the far-famed Mediterranean, of the deepest blue colour, and quite transparent, dark red rocks jutting out into it. But the line soon turns inland again winding through wooded hills, valleys, gardens, orchards of olives, and finally orange trees. At 11.25 we got to Toulon but could see very little of it. High hills rise at the back, and after leaving Toulon, the line winds along above the sea and rocks, something like the coast near Aberdeen, only with a vegetation of stone pines and olives.[38]

Campanile among olives, Menton. (Watercolour by Gabriel Carelli.)

It was a mark of high appreciation when new scenery reminded Queen Victoria of Scotland. The train rattled on through Cannes, 'a perfect mass of villas and hotels', and the scenery became 'really ideal and brilliant beyond belief'. She passed Monaco and 'Monte Carlo, which is beautifully situated and with a wonderful vegetation of aloes, palms, and orange trees laden with fruit'.

The Chalet des Rosiers, lent to the Queen by Mr Henfrey in 1882, with the old town of Menton in the background. (Watercolour by E. B. Crawley-Boevey.)

Menton was 'charmingly situated'[39] and the Chalet des Rosiers she described as 'a small villa in the Swiss style, something like the Villa Hohenlohe'.[40] This was health-resort architecture: the Villa Hohenlohe was the house in Baden-Baden which had been left to the Queen by her half-sister Feodore. The chalet was, she wrote, 'very prettily situated, out of the town, well above the sea, with Mentone to the right, close under the mountains and near a fine valley covered with olive woods'.[41] She had left Windsor at 10.15 a.m. on 14 March; it was now 'tea-time' on the 16th; not surprisingly, she was 'dreadfully hot and tired. Took tea and rested. Much unpacking . . .'[42]

Queen Victoria took to the south of France at once: 'Oh! how beautiful the deep blue sky, with the background of jagged mountains, and then the thick olive groves'. As she wrote 'white roses are trailed along the lower balcony, as well as dark purple bougainvillaea. I could write volumes on the marvellous luxuriant beauty of this southern vegetation.'[43] It was all very different from Windsor in March.

She bombarded Sir Henry Ponsonby for information: 'How long would it

'Charles Alberque, a cripple' in a watercolour by A. Forestier. It was typical of the Queen that among her souvenirs she kept a painting of this man whose difficulties, and their ingenious canine solution, she had seen for herself.

La Mortola, only ten minutes' drive from the Chalet des Rosiers, where the Queen would come to sketch.

take to drive to Ventimiglia & to Bordighera & to Monaco? Perhaps Sir Henry will make enquiries about a china manufactory near here & a Monastery. In short find out about any excursions within reach.'[44]

With horses and outriders from Milan, an English coachman and her kilted Highlander on the box, she soon became a familiar sight on the 'beautiful Corniche road, which one can only admire more and more',[45] and on the dusty byways that took her up into the valleys to see a picturesque village, a convent or a pottery, or to find a sheltered spot to take tea at the roadside, where she met few people – women with their donkeys, travelling gypsies, strolling players and once 'our washerwoman, who was so overcome at seeing me, that she knelt down in the road!'[46]

There is little of that rural charm left on the French Riviera; it was receding, and its loss was being mourned, even then. Villas and flats jostle for space and a view of the sea, the old roads are clogged with traffic and the people of Nice say they never had such winds before the autoroute cut through the massif de l'Estérel. The centre of Menton still preserves its picturesque old streets and houses and the spire of St Michael's church still rises out of it, just as it used to; but the 'fine valley' is built over and the olive woods have dwindled to a public park. The Chalet des Rosiers still exists, as luxury apartments with glitzy interiors, all marble and smoked glass, but the last patch of the garden disappeared under six new apartments in 1992. There is still a winged wheel over what used to be the stables or coach house, a reminder of Charles Henfrey's railway achievements. It seems appropriate that Queen Victoria should have stayed in two houses built with money made from the very railways which had brought her so much freedom and pleasure through her long travelling career.

There is one place, however, which does still convey the feel of the Côte d'Azur a hundred years ago, and this is the Villa Hanbury, which in the Queen's day was called La Mortola, meaning myrtle. Here Sir Thomas Hanbury, who had made his fortune in the Far East, began a garden in 1867. Its eighteen green and lovely hectares, one of the most important botanic gardens in the world, still stretch down to the sea today, hiding a villa which Queen Victoria called 'a regular little old Italian palazzo'.[47] It now belongs to the University of Genoa. You descend from the road on foot down a series of rugged terraces, surrounded all the way by huge trees, exotic shrubs and delicious smells, and can find again the atmosphere that space and luxuriant vegetation gave to the whole coastline in Queen Victoria's day.

She came at the end of winter; we are here at its beginning, when an out-of-

season peace begins to take over. The sun shines down through the pines and the white waves curl in over the rocks, a ripple of birdsong fills the air, one or two late butterflies flutter past and the faint aromatic scents of the garden are blown on the breeze. The clear light shines down through the olive trees; the sun is warm on your cheek and the breeze brushes your bare arm; Queen Victoria would never have allowed the sun on her skin, but she did remark on its exhilarating effects on mind and spirits. The Victorians, for whom the winter was the time to visit the Mediterranean, had a much more moderate response to the seasons than we, who tend to take our holidays in August.

On the terrace beside the white, barley-sugar columns of the villa, is a maze of rosemary. The bushes catch you as you pass by, and the scent, pungent, refreshing, invigorating, rises up around you. The Hanbury family were given to recording events in tablets of stone, and set in the wall of the terrace is a white marble plaque with a Latin inscription to the effect that Her Majesty came, liked what she saw, and sat there to paint it.

On the way to Nice our map-reading leaves something to be desired, and we find ourselves winding up through the village of La Turbie, only to find that Queen Victoria had followed this road too, on 5 April 1882, to within half a mile of the 'very curious old Roman ruin' of La Turbie. This vast monument, La Trophée des Alpes, was put up in 6 BC by the Emperor Augustus, to celebrate his defeat of the Ligurian tribes. Queen Victoria saw it in the condition to which it had been reduced, by barbarians who damaged it to get their own back on the Romans, by sixth-century Christians because the natives regarded it as a god, by the thirteenth century which turned it into a fortress and by the eighteenth century which blew it up. Since her day, it has been much restored, so that its silhouette once again dominates the coastline.

Of the places where Queen Victoria stayed in the south of France, the Chalet des Rosiers, the smallest, has perhaps fared the best. Some of the large hotels have come down in the world. Fashions changed and Grasse, for instance, inland from the sea, no longer needed its Grand Hotel: after the Second World War, during which it had been occupied by both sides, the building was divided into flats. Over the door is a plaque commemorating Queen Victoria's visit in 1891. The place seems to be doing its best to ignore the Citroën garage opposite, and closes its turquoise shutters to the villas which have sprung up on the hillside across the road, where the Queen would take tea in Miss Rothschild's 'paradise of a garden'.[48]

Similarly stranded by the tide of fashion, which ebbed away to the coast as people began to come for sea and sand, is the vast Hotel Regina. Dominating an

Queen Victoria starting for her afternoon drive. (Gouache by Reginald Cleaver.) It is a long time since the coronets of the outmoded Hotel Regina have been celebrated by a fanfare of trumpets.

outmoded eminence at the top of the Boulevard de Cimiez in Nice, its coronets crumbling among the palm trees, it looks like the wreck of an ambitious dream. Here the Queen spent her final spring holidays in 1897, 1898 and 1899, having had to move into it from the old Grand Hotel (now part of Nice hospital) when the Regina was built right in her view. It had no garden, so the Queen used to go just down the hill to sit out in the gardens of the Villa Liserbe. Now these gardens are all built over, and the wild and rural ways in the hinterland of 'dear beautiful Cimiez' are engulfed in suburbs.

Other places Queen Victoria tried only once or twice; Cimiez she returned to time and again, not only because in her old age she perhaps no longer had the energy to try out somewhere new but also because Cimiez offered everything. She had easy access to spectacular scenery for her daily drives; in the town at her feet were gardens and villas full of aristocracy and royalty, and since the Riviera was the terminus for so many of Europe's high born (her own son, Leopold, had died here), there were affecting memorials to visit. She obviously enjoyed the contrasts: tea one day with an empress in a white panelled drawing room hung with Chinese embroideries, two days later in a quarry at the side of the road.

At the height of the summer season today the same grandeur and high social life is still religiously adhered to. People rent or buy houses along the coast, or live in hotels for months to enjoy the parties and high social whiz that Queen Victoria was never part of but to which her invisible presence gave extra cachet. Our hotel in Cap Ferrat is one of the few still open in early winter and we had arrived without knowing that she had visited the peninsula before us, though we sense that she has. She must have the last word on the Côte d'Azur:

Drove ... to Cap Ferrat, beyond Villefranche, at the end of the point, forming one side of the harbour. It is quite beautiful. We drove past the light house and through the pine woods overhanging the sea. Took our tea there, in a lovely sheltered spot. The lights over the sea and mountains, driving home, were quite exquisite.[49]

Home? It is time to make a dash for the train; we have left very little time. The ornate pink and white buildings and the palm trees of the centre of Nice go flying by. The station looks like a German schloss, a magnificent building, a fitting temple to the most modern technology its day had to offer.

The railway, still a romantic and peaceful mode of transport, runs close to the seafront as we pull out of Nice between palm trees and on past the red rock hills with their lavender bushes, olive trees and an occasional eucalyptus. All

'Alas! my last charming drive in this paradise of nature, which I grieve to leave, as I get more attached to it every year. I shall mind returning to the sunless north, but I am so grateful for all I have enjoyed here.'

1 MAY 1899

through the mountains are bitter memorials of the Resistance and the war. We are to travel back through the landscape which Queen Victoria first set eyes on one hundred and ten years earlier. What will have happend to it?

Shades of green colour the countryside, the aloes groan with sheer delight after the recent rain, and you let your imagination glide as you smell the heat off the land. A glimpse of purple, heather-like flowers flashes past: still a hint of Scotland!

Past Toulon, and the train is speeding merrily on through rolling hills; this is Monet country, fragrant with the smell of herbs and pine needles. High, white mountains, not snow but a chalky rock, bring on grim thoughts of winter and cold ahead. We whiz through Aubagne. A fairytale castle suddenly appears through the trees, but directly in front of it is a factory. Bang! the modern age.

We reach Marseilles and the aloes are creeping on to the track. Maquis, olives and cypresses, low red roofs and distant smokestacks are followed by bamboo, umbrella pines and a petro-chemical plant (the smell seems to penetrate even the air-conditioning system). Lunch arrives on a freezing tray; cod fillets lie shivering on the plates. Outside eyesore after eyesore rolls by: clusters of tall steel tanks and large white globes, huge brown cylinders and more smokestacks, red and white like barbers' poles, obliterate the landscape. Fields of cars glitter in the sun, kilometres of fuel tanks wait in sidings. How much further can we grow? How far can we take the technology that brought Queen Victoria, and so many others, ourselves included, freedom and pleasure, without looking in front of our noses at nature and seeing what we are doing to our world?

Victoria R 1897

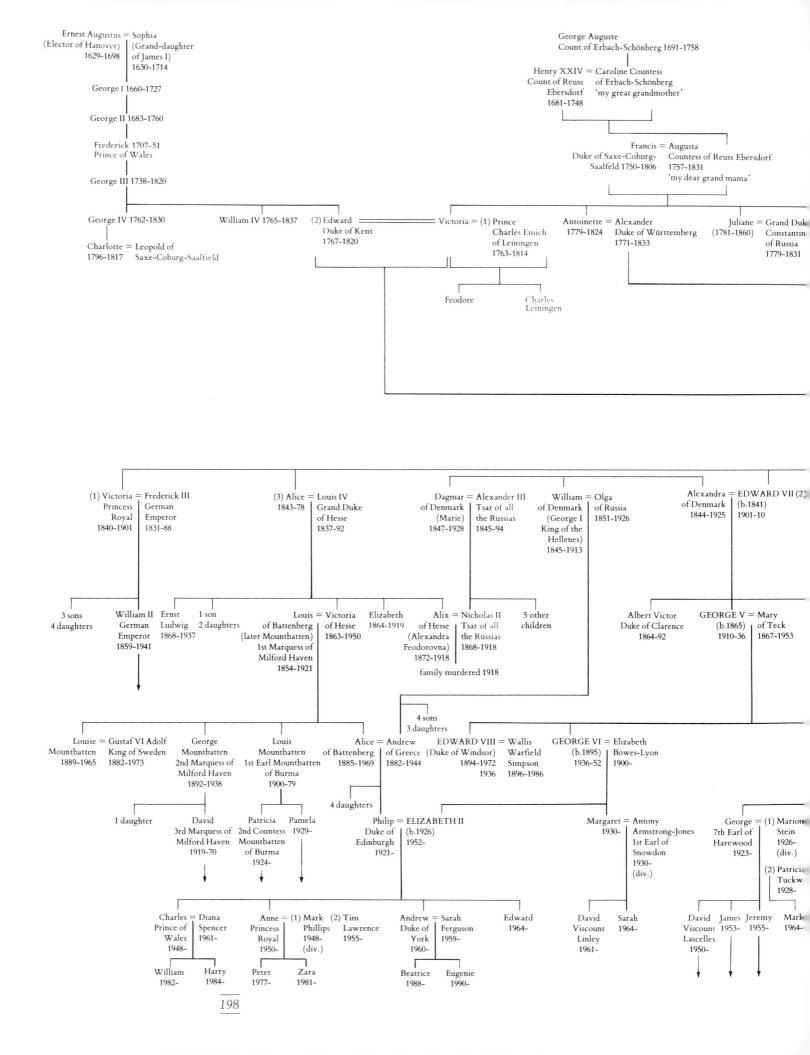

FAMILY TREE

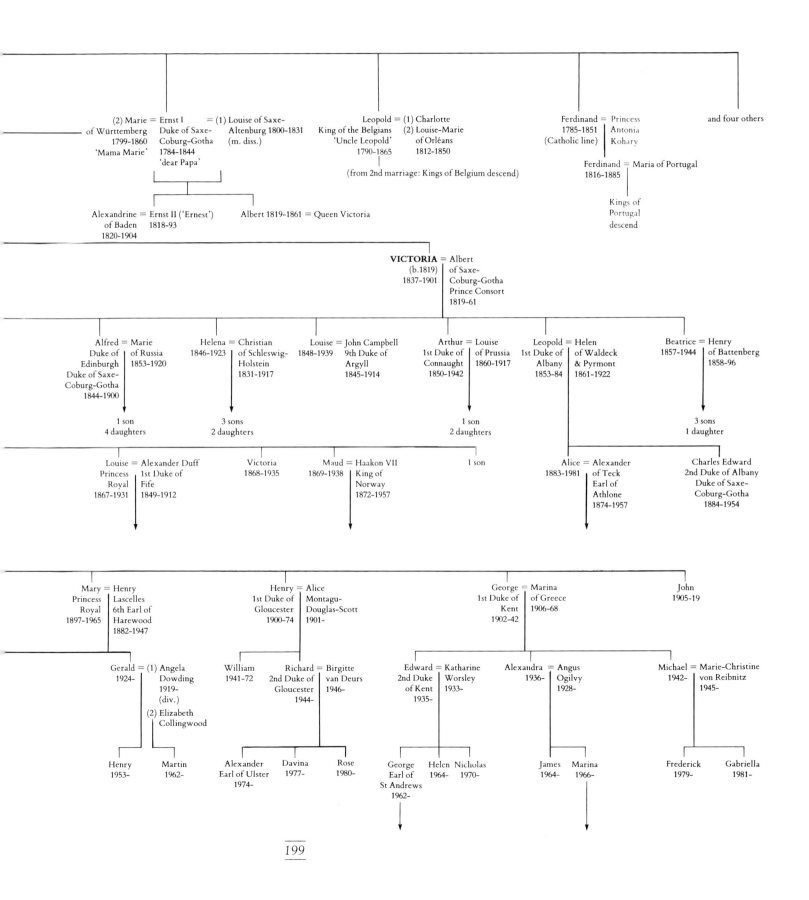

Reference Notes

Abbreviations
QVJ   Queen Victoria's Journal.
RA   Royal Archives.

For full biographical details of works cited, see page 202.

All displayed quotations are taken from Queen Victoria's Journal.

CHAPTER ONE
Her Majesty's Plans and Preparations

1 Surtees, p.97
2 RA QVJ 16 Sept 1843
3 Bolitho, p.81
4 RA Add. A24/20 16 Sept 1845
5 RA Add. A24/66 10 Sept 1858
6 RA QVJ 12 Oct 1860
7 RA Y105/32
8 *Dearest Mama*, p.114
9 RA QVJ 23 Aug 1868
10 RA QVJ 24 Aug 1868
11 RA QVJ 25 Mar 1872
12 *Dearest Mama*, p.106
13 RA QVJ 25 Mar 1872
14 Ibid.
15 Ibid.
16 RA QVJ 30 Mar 1876
17 RA L26/140
18 RA QVJ 25 Mar 1888
19 *Beloved and Darling Child*, p.66
20 RA QVJ 31 Mar 1888
21 RA QVJ 30 Mar 1882
22 *Beloved and Darling Child*, p.141
23 Ibid.
24 Ibid.
25 RA QVJ 1 Apl 1887
26 Bolitho, p.78
27 RA L26/140
28 Ibid.
29 *The New York Herald*, 26 Mar 1885
30 *The Times*, 11 Apl 1885
31 Bolitho, p.80
32 RA Y82/75
33 RA QVJ 12 Aug 1858
34 RA B19/131
35 *Beloved Mama*, p.35
36 RA QVJ 16 Mar 1894
37 Ponsonby 1951, p.53
38 Bolitho, p.80
39 Ibid.
40 RA Z279 p.3
41 Surtees, p.97
42 RA QVJ 9 Apl 1891

43 Mallet, p.44
44 Ponsonby 1951, p.52
45 RA QVJ 16 Mar 1882
46 RA Z279 p.90
47 RA Add. MS O/60
48 RA PP Vic 6050 30 Nov 1860
49 RA Add. A30/554 27 Nov 1861
50 RA Add. A30/557 3 Dec 1862
51 RA Add. A20/1236 20 Dec 1864
52 RA Add. Q1/86 4 June 1867
53 RA Add. L27 7 Aug 1874
54 RA QVJ 22 Aug 1868
55 RA QVJ 24 Apl 1888
56 Surtees, p.154
57 RA QVJ 18 Aug 1845
58 *Leaves from a Journal*, 18 Aug 1855
59 RA Add. O39
60 RA QVJ 16 Mar 1882
61 RA PP Osb. 757 Mar 1891
62 RA MOH LB I/184 6 Aug 1862
63 RA MOH LB I/186
64 RA MOH LB I/190
65 RA MOH LB I/210
66 RA QVJ 7 Aug 1868
67 RA QVJ 28 Mar 1879
68 RA QVJ 23 Apl 1879
69 RA QVJ 17 Mar 1882
70 Grihangne, p.23
71 RA A279, p.87v
72 Krueger, p.287
73 RA Z279, p.69
74 RA QVJ 5 Apl 1885
75 Ponsonby 1951, p.53
76 RA Z279, p.2
77 RA QVJ 31 Mar 1887
78 Miller, p.26
79 RA L9/96 25 Apl 1879
80 Charlot, p.255
81 RA QVJ 19 Mar 1855
82 RA QVJ 11 July 1855
83 Gavin, p.133
84 Ibid.
85 RA L1/51a Prince Leiningen to Queen Victoria 23 Mar 1876
86 Gavin, p.150
87 RA QVJ 27 Apl 1887
88 RA Add. O20
89 Ibid.
90 RA Add. O21
91 RA Add. O20
92 RA Add. O21
93 RA Add. O20
94 RA Add. O11 Colonel Phipps to Queen Victoria 14 Oct 1860
95 Ponsonby 1951, p.56

CHAPTER TWO
The Pilgrimage to Coburg, 1845

1 Surtees, p.154
2 RA Z279, p.10
3 Ibid.
4 RA Z279, p.9
5 Ibid.
6 Surtees, p.155
7 RA Z279, p.12
8 RA Z279, p.14
9 *The Journals of Dorothy Wordsworth*, ed William Knight (London, 1925), pp.430–31
10 Surtees, p.155
11 RA Z279, p.11
12 RA Z279, p.18
13 Ibid.
14 RA Z279, pp.18–19
15 RA Z279, pp.19–20
16 RA Z279, p.20
17 RA Z279, p.21
18 RA Z279, p.23
19 RA Z279, pp.20–1
20 RA Z279, p.11
21 RA Z279, p.21
22 RA Z279, p.22
23 Ibid.
24 RA Z279, p.23
25 RA Z279, p.25
26 Ibid.
27 RA Z279, p.28
28 RA Z279, pp.29–30
29 RA Z279, p.30
30 RA Z279, p.31
31 RA Z279, p.32
32 Ibid.
33 RA Z279, p.33
34 Ibid.
35 Ibid.
36 Ibid.
37 RA Z279, p.34
38 Ibid.
39 RA Z279, p.33
40 RA Z279, p.34

CHAPTER THREE
The Land of Albert's Birth, 1845

1 RA Z279, p.36
2 Ibid.
3 Ibid.
4 RA Z279, p.37
5 Ibid.
6 Marie of Roumania, p.156

7 RA Z279, p.44
8 Ibid.
9 Surtees, p.158
10 RA Z279, p.47
11 *Dearest Mama*, p.262
12 RA Z279, p.46
13 RA Z279, p.43
14 RA Z279, p.46
15 RA Z279, p.42
16 RA QVJ 24 Aug 1845
17 RA Z279, p.48
18 RA Z279, p.40
19 Ibid.
20 Ibid.
21 RA Z279, p.41
22 RA Z279, pp.37–8
23 RA Z279, p.38
24 Surtees, p.157
25 RA Z279, p.38
26 RA Z279, p.51
27 RA Z279, p.38
28 RA Z279, p.39
29 RA Z279, p.38
30 RA Z279, p.39
31 RA Z279, p.43
32 RA Z279, p.51
33 RA Z279, p.82
34 RA Z279, p.57
35 RA Z279, p.58
36 Surtees, p.161
37 RA Z279, p.58
38 RA Z279, p.59
39 RA Z279, p.60
40 RA Z279, p.62
41 Ibid.
42 Taylor, p.159
43 RA Z279, p.62
44 RA Z279, p.67
45 RA Z279, p.81
46 RA Z279, p.67
47 RA Z279, p.69–70
48 RA Z279, p.77

CHAPTER FOUR
The State Visit to Paris, 1855

1 RA QVJ 3 Dec 1851
2 RA QVJ 19 Apl 1855
3 Greville, p.156
4 *Leaves from a Journal*, 19 Apl 1855
5 *Leaves from a Journal*, 18 Aug 1855
6 Ibid.
7 Ibid.
8 Ibid.
9 Ibid.
10 Ibid.
11 *Leaves from a Journal*, 20 Aug 1855
12 Ibid.
13 Ibid.

14 Ibid.
15 Ibid.
16 *Leaves from a Journal*, 21 Aug 1855
17 Ibid.
18 Ibid.
19 Ibid.
20 Ibid.
21 RA QVJ 22 Aug 1855
22 *Leaves from a Journal*, 22 Aug 1855
23 Ibid.
24 *Leaves from a Journal*, 23 Aug 1855
25 *Leaves from a Journal*, 24 Aug 1855
26 Ibid.
27 *Leaves from a Journal*, 25 Aug 1855
28 *Leaves from a Journal*, 26 Aug 1855
29 Ibid.
30 *Leaves from a Journal*, 27 Aug 1855
31 RA QVJ 28 Aug 1855
32 RA QVJ 31 Aug 1855
33 RA QVJ 6 Aug 1868
34 Ibid.
35 RA QVJ 27 Mar 1879
36 RA QVJ 26 Mar 1879
37 RA QVJ 27 Mar 1879
38 RA QVJ 24 Mar 1891

CHAPTER FIVE
The Delightful Fortnight, Potsdam,
1858

1 *Dearest Child*, p.122
2 RA QVJ 11 Aug 1858
3 Ibid.
4 RA QVJ 12 Aug 1858
5 Ibid.
6 Ibid.
7 Ibid.
8 *Dearest Child*, p.122
9 RA QVJ 12 Aug 1858
10 RA QVJ 13 Aug 1858
11 RA QVJ 12 Aug 1858
12 Ibid.
13 RA QVJ 13 Aug 1858
14 Ibid.
15 Ibid.
16 Ibid.
17 RA QVJ 18 Aug 1858
18 Ibid.
19 RA QVJ 17 Aug 1858
20 Ibid.
21 RA QVJ 13 Aug 1858
22 RA QVJ 19 Aug 1858
23 Murray, p.140
24 Spencer, vol 1 p.103
25 RA QVJ 19 Aug 1858
26 RA QVJ 17 Aug 1858
27 RA QVJ 13 Aug 1858
28 RA QVJ 22 Aug 1858
29 Ibid.
30 *Dearest Child*, p.148

31 RA QVJ 16 Aug 1858
32 Ibid.
33 RA QVJ 24 April 1888
34 Ibid.

CHAPTER SIX
The Late Holidays, 1861–1899

1 RA QVJ 4 Oct 1862
2 RA QVJ 8 Sept 1863
3 Reid (ed) *Playfair*, p.176
4 RA QVJ 30 Mar 1880
5 Ibid.
6 Ibid.
7 RA QVJ 1 Apl 1880
8 RA QVJ 24 Apl 1895
9 RA QVJ 6 May 1884
10 RA QVJ 17 Apl 1884
11 RA QVJ 28 Apl 1885
12 RA QVJ 23 Apl 1885
13 Duff, p.93
14 RA QVJ 29 Apl 1885
15 Ibid.
16 RA QVJ 29 Mar 1879
17 Ibid.
18 RA QVJ 28 Mar 1879
19 Ibid.
20 *Beloved Mama*, p.41
21 RA QVJ 29 Mar 1879
22 Ibid.
23 *Beloved Mama*, p.40
24 Ibid.
25 RA QVJ 7 Apl 1879
26 *Beloved Mama*, p.39
27 *Beloved Mama*, p.41
28 RA QVJ 6 Apl 1879
29 RA QVJ 15 Apl 1879
30 RA L9/91
31 Ponsonby, p.286
32 RA QVJ 30 Mar 1879
33 RA QVJ 8 Apl 1879
34 *Letters of Queen Victoria*, 2nd series, vol 3,
   p.14
35 Ponsonby, p.284
36 RA QVJ 5 Apl 1879
37 RA QVJ 29 Mar 1879
38 RA QVJ 16 Mar 1882
39 Ibid.
40 Ibid.
41 Ibid.
42 Ibid.
43 RA QVJ 16 Mar 1882
44 Ponsonby, p.285
45 RA QVJ 5 Apl 1882
46 RA QVJ 27 Mar 1882
47 RA QVJ 25 Mar 1882
48 RA QVJ 26 Mar 1891
49 RA QVJ 6 Apl 1895

Select Bibliography

BAEDEKER, K. *Deutschland und das Österreichische; Handbuch für Reisende* (Koblenz, 1859)

BOLITHO (ed) *The Prince Consort and his brother* (London, 1933)

BUCKLE, GEORGE EARL (ed) *The Letters of Queen Victoria*, 2nd series, vol 3 (London, 1928)

The Letters of Queen Victoria, 3rd series, vol 1 (London 1930)

CHARLOT, MONICA *Victoria the Young Queen* (Oxford UK & Cambridge USA, 1991)

DUFF, DAVID *Hessian Tapestry* (London, 1967)

Victoria Travels (London, 1970)

FULFORD, ROGER (ed) *Dearest Child; Letters between Queen Victoria and the Princess Royal 1858–1861* (London, 1964)

Dearest Mama; Letters between Queen Victoria and The Crown Princess of Prussia 1865–1871 (London, 1968)

Beloved Mama; Private Correspondence of Queen Victoria and the German Crown Princess 1878–1885) (London, 1981)

GAVIN, C. M. *Royal Yachts* (London, 1932)

GRIHANGNE, ROGER *Queen Victoria in Grasse* trans and ed David Lockie (Grasse, 1991)

KRUEGER, INGEBORG 'Queen Victorias Besuch am Rhein', in *Vom Zauber des Rheins Ergriffen*, eds Klaus Honnef, Klaus Weschenfelder, Irene Haberland (Munich, 1992)

LONGFORD, ELIZABETH *Victoria RI* (London, 1984)

MALLET, VICTOR *Life with Queen Victoria: Marie Mallet's Letters from Court 1887–1901* (London, 1968)

MARIE OF ROUMANIA, QUEEN *The Story of My Life* (New York, 1923)

MILLER, WILLIAM, *Wintering in the Riviera* (London, 1879)

MURRAY, JOHN (ed) *Handbook for North Germany and the Rhine* (London, 1886)

PAGET, WALBURGA LADY *Embassies of other days* (London, 1923)

PONSONBY, ARTHUR *Henry Ponsonby, Queen Victoria's Private Secretary: His life from his Letters* (London, 1943)

PONSONBY, SIR FREDERICK *Recollections of Three Reigns* (London, 1951)

RAMM, AGATHA (ed) *Beloved and Darling Child; Last letters between Queen Victoria and her eldest daughter 1886–1901* (London, 1990)

REID, WEMYSS *Memoirs of Lyon Playfair* (London, 1899)

SAUNDERS, EDITH *A Distant Summer* (London, 1947)

SPENCER, E. *Sketches of Germany and the Germans*, vol 1 (London, 1836)

STRACHEY, LYTTON and ROGER FULFORD (eds) *The Greville Memoirs 1814–1860* vol 7 (London, 1938)

SURTEES, VIRGINIA *Charlotte Canning; Lady in Waiting to Queen Victoria and wife of the first Viceroy of India 1817–1861* (London, 1975)

TAYLOR, SHEPHARD THOMAS *An Historical Tour, or, The Early Ancestors of the Prince of Wales, of the House of Wettin* (London, 1884)

VICTORIA, QUEEN *Leaves from a Journal being a record of the Visit of the Emperor and Empress of the French to the Queen and of the Queen and HRH the Prince Consort to the Emperor of the French* (private circulation, 1855)

Picture Acknowledgements

The authors and publishers would like to thank the staff of the Royal Archives and Royal Library, Windsor, and the Royal Collection for their help in providing information and material for this book. The illustrations used are as follows: The Royal Archives © 1993 Her Majesty The Queen: pages 1, 14, 15, 20, 22, 24 (below), 26, 27, 29, 31, 35, 36, 38, 40, 43, 88, 124 (above and below), 125, 167, 174 (right); The Royal Collection © 1993 Her Majesty The Queen: pages 2, 17, 18, 19, 23, 24 (above), 30, 33, 39, 42, 44, 45, 51, 54 (above), 57, 59, 63, 64, 66, 68, 75, 78, 79, 81, 83, 85, 86, 91, 92, 93 (right), 95 (above), 97, 98, 101, 102, 103, 104 (right), 106 (above), 107 (below), 109 (left), 110, 112, 114, 117, 118, 126, 127 (above), 127 (below), 128, 129 (below), 132, 134–5, 140, 141, 143, 144, 145, 147, 148, 153, 154, 158, 163, 164 (right), 178, 180, 182, 184, 185, 186, 189, 190, 191, 192, 194.

© Her Royal Highness The Duchess of York: pages 70, 93 (right), 104 (left), 145, 204.

Acknowledgement and thanks are also due to the following museums and organizations for permission to reproduce pictures in their collections: The Illustrated London News Picture Library: pages 16, 25, 37, 54 (below), 56, 62, 67 (below), 74, 108, 119, 121, 129 (above), 136–7, 165; The Bridgeman Art Library: endpapers, pages 120, 122, 123; Schlossmuseum Darmstadt, Residenz Schloss: pages 168, 173.

The following photographs are by Robin Matthews © Weidenfeld and Nicolson: pages 7, 9, 11, 12, 13, 21, 46, 49, 50, 52, 55, 58, 60, 65, 67 (above), 69, 71, 72, 73, 76–7, 87, 90, 94, 95 (below), 96, 100, 105, 106 (below), 107 (above), 109 (right), 111, 115, 139, 146, 149, 150, 155, 156, 159, 160, 161, 164 (left), 172, 174 (left), 176, 179, 181, 183, 187, 193, 195.

Weidenfeld and Nicolson Archive: page 197

Index

Numbers in *italic* indicate captions.
QV refers to Queen Victoria,
PA to Prince Albert.

Aberdeen, Lord 32
Aix-la-Chapelle 53–4, 138
Aix-les-Bains 24, *24*, 27, 28, *28*, 32, 38, 39, 42, 48
Alberque, Charles *192*
Albert Edward, Prince of Wales 20, 34, 38, *39*, *40*, 84, *87*, 123, 130, 132, 162
Albert of Saxe-Coburg-Gotha, Prince Consort: and souvenir albums *10*, 14; timetable of travels 16, 18, 19, 20; death 20–1, 166, 177; statue in Coburg *21*, 99; QV's attitude to travel after his death 22, 30; makes plans and preparations 28, 29; and travelling companions 32, 34; and mode of transport *40*, 41, 43, 44; coat of arms *47*; at Brühl 56, 58, 62; as student *57*, 57; at Stolzenfels 63, *65*, 69, 71; at Mainz 75; points out places of interest to QV 82; arrives in Coburg 84, *85*; love for father 88; in the Ehrenburg *94*, *96*, 97; and entertainments in Coburg 98; at the Veste 100; at the Rosenau *104*, *105*, 108, 109, *109*, *110*, *111*, 112, *113*; at Rodach 114; at Reinhardsbrunn *117*, *119*; likes Empress Eugénie 123; visits Paris 123, 128, *129*, 131, *133*; journey to Potsdam 138; at Babelsberg 142, 145, 151; at review in Lustgarten 152; at Klein Glienicke 162
Albert the Unnatural 116
albums 10, *10*, 13–14, *14*
Alexander I, Tsar of Russia 86
Alexandrine of Baden, Princess 89
Alfred, Prince, Duke of Edinburgh and Saxe-Coburg-Gotha 27, 30, 34
Alice, Princess 166, 169, 170, 171, 172
Alice of Battenberg, Princess 171
Alix of Hesse, Princess *167*, 169, 174, *174*
Alte Palais, Darmstadt 170
Anson, George 32, 112
Antwerp 19, 36, 40, 41, 138
Arona 188, 189
Arthur of Connaught, Prince *28*, 34
Aschaffenburg 79
Aubagne 197
Audy *120*
Augusta of Saxe-Weimar, Princess 144–5

Auguste Reuss zu Ebersdorf, Princess, Duchess of Saxe-Coburg-Saalfeld (QV's grandmother) 85, 177
Augustus, Emperor 195
Augustusburg (formerly Schloss Brühl) *see* Schloss Brühl

Babelsberg *see* Schloss Babelsberg
Baden, Grand Duke of 109
Baden-Baden *22*, 22–3, 28, 45, 191
Balmoral 19, 28, 112
Bamberg 82
Banz Abbey 82
Basel 42
Battle of Flowers, Grasse 24
Baveno 37, 42, 180–9
Beatrice, Princess 15, *24*, *28*, 32, 38, 88, 165, *167*, 182, 185, 188
Becker, Auguste *140*
Beethoven, statue of *56*, 57
Bensheim 177
Berlin 20, 27, 30, 34, 60, 138, 142, 162, 163–5, *165*
Berlin Wall 143
Bernascon, Monsieur 38, 39
Biarritz 24
Bingen 75
Bismarck, Prince 27, 70
Black Forest 23
Bois de Boulogne *120*, 128
Bonn 40, 48, 49, *56*, 56, 57, *57*, 62
Boppard 73
Borromean Islands 180, 184
Boulogne 14, 16, 40, 45, 123–4, *124*, *125*, 133
Branca family 9, 183, 189
Brandenburg Gate 163–4
Braunshardt *see* Schloss Braunshardt
Breidenbach, William 140
Breidenbacherhof 140
Brown, Jon 188
Bruckner, Max *83*
Bruges 18
Brühl *see* Schloss Brühl

Calais-Douvres (steamship) 45
Callenberg, the 114
Callow, William *118*
Cannes 24, 41, 190
Canning, Lady 32, 35, 61, *68*, 92, 108, 116
Cap Ferrat 196
Carelli, Gabriel *24*, *180*, *182*, *185*, 190

Carlone, Carlo *51*
Caroline of Erbach, Princess (QV's great-grandmother) 177, *178*
carriages 36–8
Cart (valet) 32
Casimir, Johann, first Duke of Saxe-Coburg 101, 102
Catherine the Great of Russia 85–6
Chalet des Rosiers, Menton 190, 191, *191*, 192, 195
Chambéry 24
Champ de Mars, Paris 132, *132*, 137
Champs Élysées, Paris 128
Charlemagne 53–4
Charles X, King of France 130
Charles of Prussia, Prince 162
Charlotte, Princess 86–7
Charlottenburg, Berlin 163, *164*, 165
Château d'Eu 16, *19*
Cherbourg *43*, 45
Cimiez, 27, *27*, 39, *47*, 190, 196
Clark, Francis *167*
Clarke, Sir James 32
Cleaver, Reginald *195*
Clemens Auguste, Archbishop-Elector of Cologne, *51*, 53, 55, 61
Coburg *85*, *92*, *93*, *101*; QV's sketches of *13*, *93*; QV and PA visit (1845) 19, 28, 32, 35–6, 40, 83, 84–103; QV and PA visit (1860) 20, 41, 47, 166; QV visits (1862) 21; statue of PA in *21*, 99; QV visits (1894) 27, 41; PA plans journey 34; regimental costumes 79; *see also* Callenberg; Ehrenburg Palace; Rosenau; Veste
Coburg, House of 84–9, 114
Cologne 36, 40, 48, 49, 53, 54, 56, 57–8
Communards 136
Constantine of Russia, Grand Duke 85–6
Corden, W. 86–7
Corniche road 190, 192
Côte d'Azur 190–7
courier, royal 34–5
Crawford, Lady 23
Crawley-Boevey, E.B. *191*
Crystal Palace 130

Dallemagne, Adolphe *127*
Dannhauser, Josef *111*
Darmstadt 42, 166–71, *173*, 177; old schloss *168*, *169*, *170*, *173*

Davoust, Marshal 53
Deutz 34, 38
Diets, Arthur *32*
Disraeli, Prime Minister 28
Dolphin (vessel) 36
Dosse, Ernest 35
Drachenfels 62, *62*
Dubofe, Claude Marie *123*
Düsseldorf 138, 140, *140*

Edinburgh, Duke of *171*
Edward, Duke of Kent 16, 87
Ehrenbreitstein 69, 75
Ehrenburg Palace *86*, 87, *91*, *94*, *95*, *96*, *97*;
    visit to 84–99
Eiffel Tower 137
Einsiedeln 82
Eisenhausen 114
Elisabeth, Queen of Prussia 55, 66, 70
Elizabeth II, Queen *52*, 61
Elizabeth of Hesse, Princess *169*
Ernst I, Duke of Saxe-Coburg-Saalfeld
    (PA's father) 87–9, 93, 94, *95*, 97–8, 100,
    103, 111, *114*, 116, *117*
Ernst II, Duke of Saxe-Coburg-Gotha
    (Ernest, PA's brother) 39, 84, 89, *96*, 98,
    109, 112, 113
Ernst Ludwig of Hesse, Prince 169, *171*; as
    Hereditary Grand Duke of Hesse *167*
Eu, Forest of *18*
Eugénie, Empress *120*, 122–3, *123*, *124*, 129,
    133, 136
Exposition des Beaux Arts, Paris 128

Fairy (tender) 40, *62*, 74, *75*
Feodore, Princess of Hohenlohe-
    Langenburg 22, *22*, 23, *191*
Ferdinand, King Consort of Portugal 89
Fiesole 23
Flandrin, Hippolyte *122*
Florence 23, *23*, 30, *31*
Flushing 53, 138
Folkestone 45
Forestier, A. *23*, *192*
Fort, S. *18*
Fournier, F. de *127*
Francia, L. T. *42*
Franco-Prussian War 22, 136
Frankfurt 34, 38, 41, 79, 167
Franz Anton, Duke of Saxe-Coburg-
    Saalfeld 84
Franz Joseph, Emperor of Austria 93
Frederick the Bitten 117
Frederick the Great 142, 153, 154, 155, *156*,
    157
Frederick William II, King of Prussia 151
Frederick William IV, King of Prussia 19,
    20, 38, 40, 41, *47*, 51, 53, 56, *56*, 59, 61, 65,
    66, 70
Frederick William, Prince of Prussia (later
    Emperor Frederick III, known as Fritz)
    20, 27, 70, 138, 159, 163, 164, 165, *165*

'Fritz' *see* Frederick William, Prince of
    Prussia
Fulda 34
Furca 22

Gainsborough, Lady 32
Geneva 42
Genoa, Duchess of *185*
George I, King of England 141
George Auguste, Count of Erbach-
    Schönberg *179*
Ghent 18
Girard, Dominique 59, 60
Girardet, Karl *129*
Glienicke Bridge *143*, 144, *144*, *145*, 162
Gotha 19, 32, 34, 113, *114*, 117–8
Gourdon 48
Graeb, C. 66, *141*, *143*, *147*, *148*, *149*, *155*, *163*
Grand Hotel, Grasse *24*
Grand Opéra, Paris 130
Grand Trianon 129
Grasse 24, *24*, 34, 35, 36, 37, *37*, *38*, 38, 39,
    48, 190, 195
Gravesend 138
Greenhythe 36
Grévy, President of France 137
Griesheim, Baron 47

Hameau 129
Hanbury, Sir Thomas 192, 195
Hanover 141
Hansel, William 38, *39*
Hasselbrinck, Ferdinand 111
Hattersheim 79
Havel, the *143*, 144, 149
Heiligenberg, Schloss 177
Henfrey, Charles 37, *180*, *181*, *183*, 190, *191*,
    192
Henrietta of England 126
Henry VI, King of England 124
Henry of Battenberg, Prince *28*, *167*
Herrenhausen 141
Hildburghausen 114
Höhe, C. *57*
horses 36–7
Hotel Bellevue, Baveno *180*
Hotel Belle Vue, Cologne 36
Hotel Bellevue, Deutz 34
Hotel d'Angleterre, Frankfurt 34
Hotel de l'Europe, Aix-les-Bains 28, 38
Hotel de l'Europe, Mainz 78
Hotel de Ville, Paris *32*, 131, 136–7
Hotel Furca 22
Hotel Regina, Nice *194*, 195, 195–6
hotels 38; *see also* names of hotels
Huth, Franz *168*
Hyères 24, 190

Illustrated London News, The 37, *54*, 56
Irène of Hesse, Princess 169, 174
Isola dei Pescatori *182*, *184*
Italy, King and Queen of *185*

Jacquot (donkey) 38
Jägerhof 138, *140*
James II, King of England 133
Juliane of Saxe-Coburg-Saalfeld, Princess
    86

Kanné, Joseph Julius 34–5, *164*
Kappellan 63
Kitzingen 82
Klein Glienicke 162–3, *163*
Kloster Ebrach 82
Koblenz 40, 62, 63, 69, 75
Kranichstein 166–8
Kröh, Heinrich *173*

La Mortola (Villa Hanbury) 192, *192*, 195
La Muette 133
La Turbie 195
Lac du Bourget 27
Laecken 19, 21
Lahneck 69
Lahnstein 69
Lamartine 27
Lami, Eugene *19*
Landesburg, Schloss 116
Landseer, Sir Edwin 38
Lange Brücke 152
Le Nôtre 126, 137
Le Tréport 16, 19
Lengfurt 80
Lenné, Peter Joseph 59, 144, 151, 157
Leopold, Prince 23, 34, 196
Leopold of Saxe-Coburg, King of Belgium
    15, 18, 19, 20, 21, 29, 36, 53, *85*, 86–7, 138
Lewis the Leaper 116
Lichtenfels 41
Lind, Jenny 58, 66
Liszt, Franz 58
Liverpool, Lord 32
Locarno 184
Löhlein (servant) 32
Lorelei 74
Lorne, Marquess of *28*
Louis III, Grand Duke of Hesse-Darmstadt
    172
Louis XIV, King of France 126, 128, 129
Louis XV, King of France 133
Louis XVI, King of France 130, 131, 133
Louis of Battenberg, Prince 171, 177
Louis of Hesse, Prince 166; as Louis IV
    Hereditary Grand Duke of Hesse 170,
    172
Louis-Philippe, King of France 16, *18*, 19,
    45, 120, 129, 130
Louise, Queen of Prussia 175
Louise of Orléans 87
Louise of Saxe-Altenburg, Princess (PA's
    mother) 88, 111
Louvre 125, 128, 131
Lucerne 22
luggage 35–8
Lumley, A. 24

Index

Luna Marina *185*
Lustgarten, Potsdamer Schloss 152–3, *153*
Luther, Martin 100, 101–2, *103*

Maggiore, Lake 23, *30*, 180
Main, River 80, 82
Mainz 40, 41, 75, *78*
Mainz, Battle of 175
Maison Mottet (renamed Villa Victoria), Aix-les Bains 38, *39*
Maltzahn, Freiherr von 175, 176
Mansart, Jules-Hardouin 126
Margaret of Connaught, Princess *28*
Maria da Gloria, Queen of Portugal 89
Marie Antoinette, Queen of France 126, 128, 129–30, 131
Marie von Württemberg, Duchess of Coburg (PA's stepmother) 20, 88, 89
Marie-Louise of Austria, Princess 126
Marienberg 80
Marseilles 190, 197
Matterhorn 22
Max, Michael *159*, *164*
May of Hesse, Princess 169
Medici, Catherine de 130
Meiningen 116
Menton 23, 27, 34, 37, 190, *190*, *191*, 191, 192
Mergozzo *186*
Meyerbeer, Giacomo 58, 66
Milan 37, 180, 188, 192
Monaco 190
Mönchroden *83*
Monte Carlo 23–4, 190
Monza 185
Morandi, Teresa 189, *189*
Morel-Fatio, Antoine Leon *16*
Moritz Kirche, Coburg 99

Napoleon I, Emperor 53, 126, 128, 130, 132, *133*, 175, 190
Napoleon III, Emperor 40, 120, 122, *122*, 124, 128, *129*, 130, 131, 132, 133, 136, *136*
Neues Palais, Darmstadt 170, 171
Neues Palais, Sans Souci *159*, *161*; visit to 157–62
Neuhof, Schloss 83
Neumann, Balthasar 52, 80, 81, 82
New York Herald, The 28, 38
Nice 27, *43*, 190, 192, 195, 196
Nikolaikirche, Potsdam 152
Nôtre Dame, Paris 128

Oberlahnstein 69
Osborne House 19, 35, 112
Ostend *42*
Osterwald, G. *63*

Palais de Justice, Paris 128
Palais de l'Industrie, Paris 128
Paris, *13*, 20, 32, 34, 35, 40, 120–37; view of (1855) *136*; *see also* names of places of interest in Paris

Patricia of Connaught, Princess *28*
Penley, E. A. *44*
Pension Wallis, Lucerne 22
Persius, Ludwig 144
Petit Trianon *129*, 129
Pfalz 74
Pfaueninsel 149, *151*
Phipps, Sir Charles 47
Piazza Michelangelo, Florence 23
Pischek 66
Pitti Palace, Florence 23
Place de la Concorde, Paris 128, 130–1
Ponsonby, Sir Henry 188, 191–2
Ponte Vecchio, Florence 23
Potsdam *141*; visit to 20, 138–65; *see also* names of places of interest in Potsdam
Potsdamer Schloss 152–3, *153*
presents 47

railways 40, *40*, 41–2, *43*
Reinhardsbrunn *114*, *117*, *118*; visits to 21, 36, 39, 47, 116–9
Renié-Grétry, André-Marie 88
Residenz, Würzburg 80–1, *81*
Reuss Ebersdorff, Prince 177
Reynolds, Elizabeth 34
Rhine, River 40, 57, 62, 63, 64, 65, 68, 69, 71, 74, 75
Rhône, River *20*, 22
Riparia, V. *184*
Rochefoucauld, Baron de la 24
Rodach 114
Rome 34
Rosenau, the *104*, 105, *106*, 107, *108*, *109*, *110*, *111*; visit to 19, 21, 48, 104–113
Rosenhohe, Darmstadt 169–70
Rothbart 85, 91, 102, *103*
Rothbart, F. *95*, 106, *107*, 109, *110*, 117
Rothbart, T. *101*
Royal George (royal yacht) 43
Ruinenberg, Potsdam 154

St Cloud, Palace of *126*, *127*, 128; visit to 124–8; no longer exists 137
St Germain, Palace of 133
St Gotthard Pass 22, 34
St Petersburg 34, 86
Sainte Catherine à Garde Chasse *18*
Sainte Chapelle, Paris 128
Sans Souci *155*, *157*; visit to 153–7; *see also* Neues Palais, Sans Souci
Sarah, Duchess of York *see* York, Sarah, Duchess of
Sasso del Ferro *182*
Scheuren, C. *75*
Schilbach, H. *78*
Schinkel, Karl Friedrich 65, 88, 111, 144
Schloss Babelsberg *138*, *141*, *143*, *147*, *148*, *149*, 151; visit to 20, 30, 142–51, 152, 159
Schloss Braunshardt *172*, *173*, 176; visit to 172–6

Schloss Brühl *39*, *49*, 51, *52*, 54, *55*, *58*, *59*, *60*; visits to 35, 38, 40, 48–61, 62, 65, 152
Schloss Heiligenberg 177
Schloss Landesburg 116
Schloss Neuhof 83
Schloss Schönberg 177, *178*, 178–9, *179*
Schneider, H.J. 99
Schönberg *see* Schloss Schönberg
Scoppio del Carro 23
Scotland 43, 190, 197
Seligenstadt 79
servants 32, 34–5, 39
Simplon, the *186*, 189
sketchbooks 14–15; pictures by QV *13*, *104*, *124*, *128*, *144*, *186*, *189*
Sophia, Electress of Hanover 141
Spessart, the 79–80
Stolzenfels 47, *63*, 65, 66, 68, *69*, *73*; visits to 20, 40, 62–73, 74, 152
Strack, Heinrich 144
Strasbourg 22

Teckely (servant) 34
telegraph 39
Thomas, G.H. *153*
Thomas, R. *132*
Thüringer Railway 41
Thüringer Wald 21, 38, 48, 83, *101*, 116, 119
Tiepolo 80
Times, The 28, 39
Toce, River *186*
Toulon 190, 197
transport 40–5
travelling companions 32, 34–5
Tresserve 27
Tuileries, Palace of the 128, 130–1, 136, *136*

Uffizi, Florence 23

Versailles *120*, 129, 133, 137
Veste, the 100, *101*, *102*, *103*, *112*; visit to 100–3
Viardot, Madame 66
Victoria, Princess Royal (Vicky): marries Frederick William of Prussia 20, 138, 165; QV visits (1858) 20, 138, 142, 145, *151*, 151, 157; at Coburg 20; QV's responses to suggestions 22, 23; visits Paris (1855) *40*, 123, 133; difficulties in Prussia 151; likes Neues Palais 159; QV visits (1888) 163, *164*, 165; QV writes about Switzerland 184; loses son 185
Victoria, Queen *16*, 18, *19*, 23, *24*, 27, *28*, 31, 37, 38, 85, *120*, 129, 133, *153*, 165, *167*; records of travels 10–15; timetable of travels 16–24; and government during absence 28; choice of season 28; public welcome abroad 28–31; travels incognito 30; travelling companions 32–5; takes many things on travels 35–8; preparations at places prior to arrival of 38–9; modes of transport 40–5; buys

present for hosts 47; coat of arms 47; at Brühl 48–61; at Stolzenfels 62–73; journey from Stolzenfels to Coburg 74–83; at Ehrenburg Palace 84–99; visits Veste in Coburg 100–3; visits Rosenau 104–113; journey to Reinhardsbrunn and Gotha 114–9; state visit to Paris 120–37; at Potsdam 138–65; at Darmstadt 166–71; at Braunshardt 172–6; at Schloss Schönberg 177–9; at Villa Clara, Baveno 180–9; visits Côte d'Azur 190–7; pictures by *13, 15, 30, 104, 112, 124, 128, 144, 186, 189*; illustrations of her journal *15, 20, 24, 88*
Victoria and Albert I (royal yacht) *42*, 43
Victoria and Albert II (royal yacht) *44*, 44–5, 138
Victoria and Albert Museum 61
Victoria of Hesse, Princess (later Princess Louis of Battenburg) *167, 169, 171, 174*, 177
Victoria of Saxe-Coburg (QV's mother) 16, 87

Vierzehn Heiligen church 82
Villa Clara, Baveno *180, 181, 182, 183*; visit to 37, 180–9
Villa Delmar *see* Villa Hohenlohe
Villa Edelweiss, Cannes 24
Villa Fabbricotti, Florence 23, *31*
Villa Friesenberg, Baden-Baden *22*
Villa Hanbury *see* La Mortola
Villa Hohenlohe (formerly Villa Delmar), Baden-Baden 23, 191
Villa Liserbe, Cimiez *27*, 39, 196
Villa Palmieri, Fiesole 23
Villa Victoria (Maison Mottet), Aix-les-Bains 38, 39

Wagland, Mr (coachman) 36
Ward, E.M. *133*
Wegelin, A. *39, 51, 59*
William I, seventh King of Prussia, first German Emperor (Vicky's father-in-law) 70, 144–5, *151*, 163
William II, ninth King of Prussia and third

German Emperor (son of Vicky and Fritz) 20, 70, *165*
Windsor 10, *10*, 15, 120, *122*, 130, 133, 145, 191
Winterhalter, Franz Xaver 84
Woolwich 40
Wordsworth, Dorothy 57–8
Württemberg, Marie von, Duchess of Coburg (PA's stepmother) 20, 88, 89
Würzburg 35, 40, 48, 80, 80–1, *81*, 82
Wylde, Colonel 32, *126*

yachts, royal *42*, 43–5
York, Sarah, Duchess of 7; at Baveno *9*; at Windsor *10*; at Brühl *52*; at Stolzenfels *71, 73*; above the Rhine *76*; at Ehrenburg *87, 94*; at Rosenau *105, 111*; at Babelsberg *138, 149*; in Neues Palais, Sans Souci *161*; at Braunshardt *172*; at Schönberg *179*; sketches by *70, 93, 104, 145*

Zouaves *13, 125*

First published in Great Britain in 1993 by
George Weidenfeld and Nicolson Ltd
Orion House, 5 Upper St Martin's Lane, London WC2H 9EA

ISBN: 297 83195 X

Designed by Harry Green

Phototypeset by Keyspools Ltd, Golborne, Lancs
Colour separations by Newsele Litho Ltd
Printed in Great Britain

ENDPAPERS Queen Victoria driving with the Empress
Eugénie through the Bois de Boulogne.
(Oil painting by Audy.)
PAGE 1 A detail from the illuminated route of the Queen's
train journey from Boulogne to Paris, 1855 (see page 14).
FRONTISPIECE Arrival of Queen Victoria at Boulogne-sur-Mer
(Louis Armand).
PAGE 197 Diamond Jubilee portrait of
Queen Victoria, signed and approved by her
(Etching, A. Forestier 1897).